THE ROCKS
CRY OUT

THE ROCKS CRY OUT

deborah de jong

ISBN: 978-0-9974659-0-7

Published and printed in the United States of America by the Write Place, Inc. For more information, please contact:

the Write Place, Inc.
709 Main Street, Suite 2
Pella, Iowa 50219
www.thewriteplace.biz

Cover and interior design by Alexis Thomas, the Write Place.

Copies of this book may be ordered from the Write Place online at
www.thewriteplace.biz/bookstore.

DEDICATION

This book is dedicated to my photographer father, who inspires me to be the best photographer I can be; my husband for putting up with my spontaneous whims as a photographer; and my family and friends, who have been instrumental in encouraging me on this journey.

A special thank you goes to my dear friend Ann for her assistance in this endeavor. Her expertise and wisdom is greatly appreciated.

TABLE OF CONTENTS

1

And God Saw That It Was Good

"In the beginning, God created the heavens and the earth . . . And God saw that it was good."

GENESIS 1:1-24 (NIV)

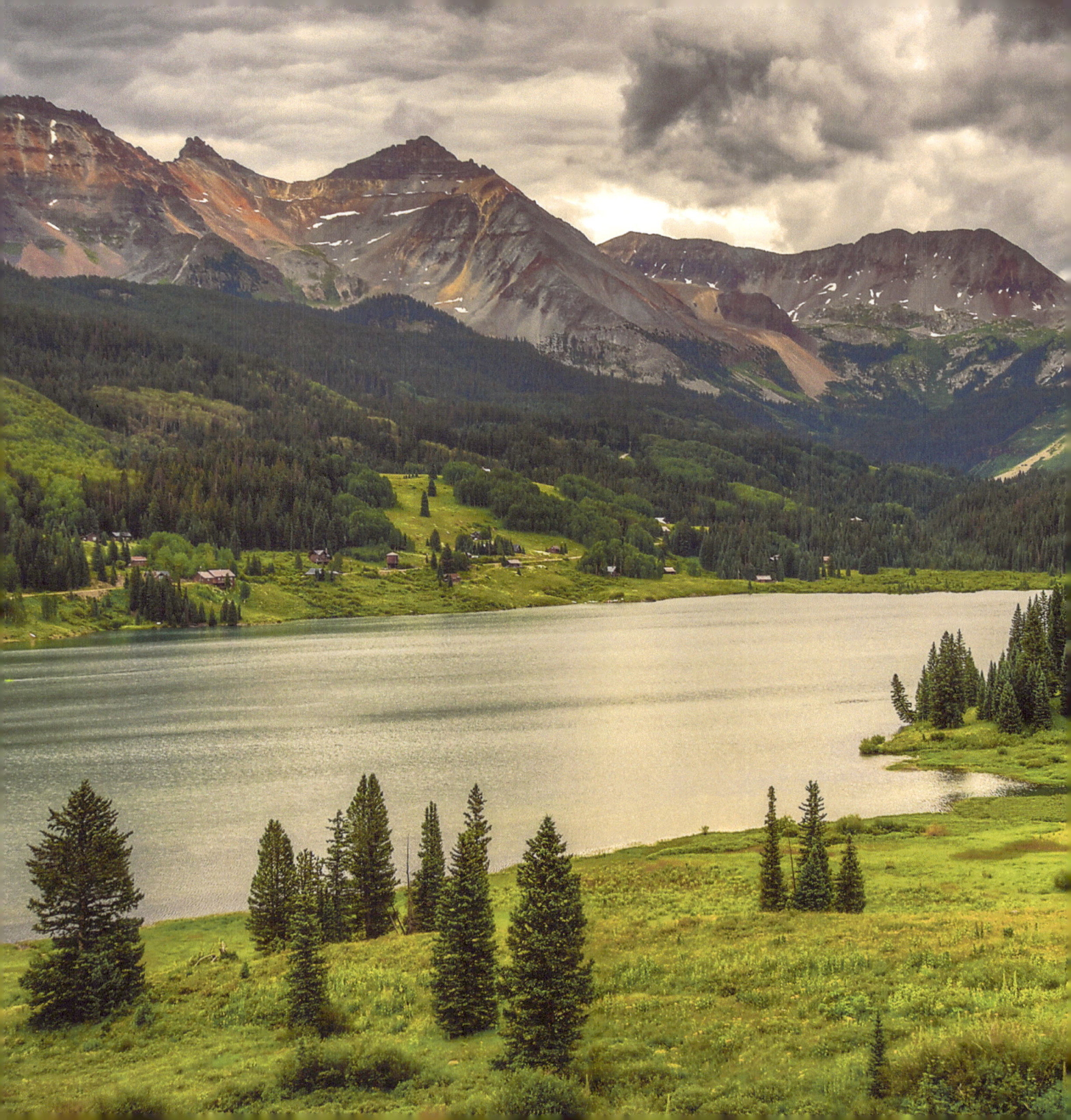

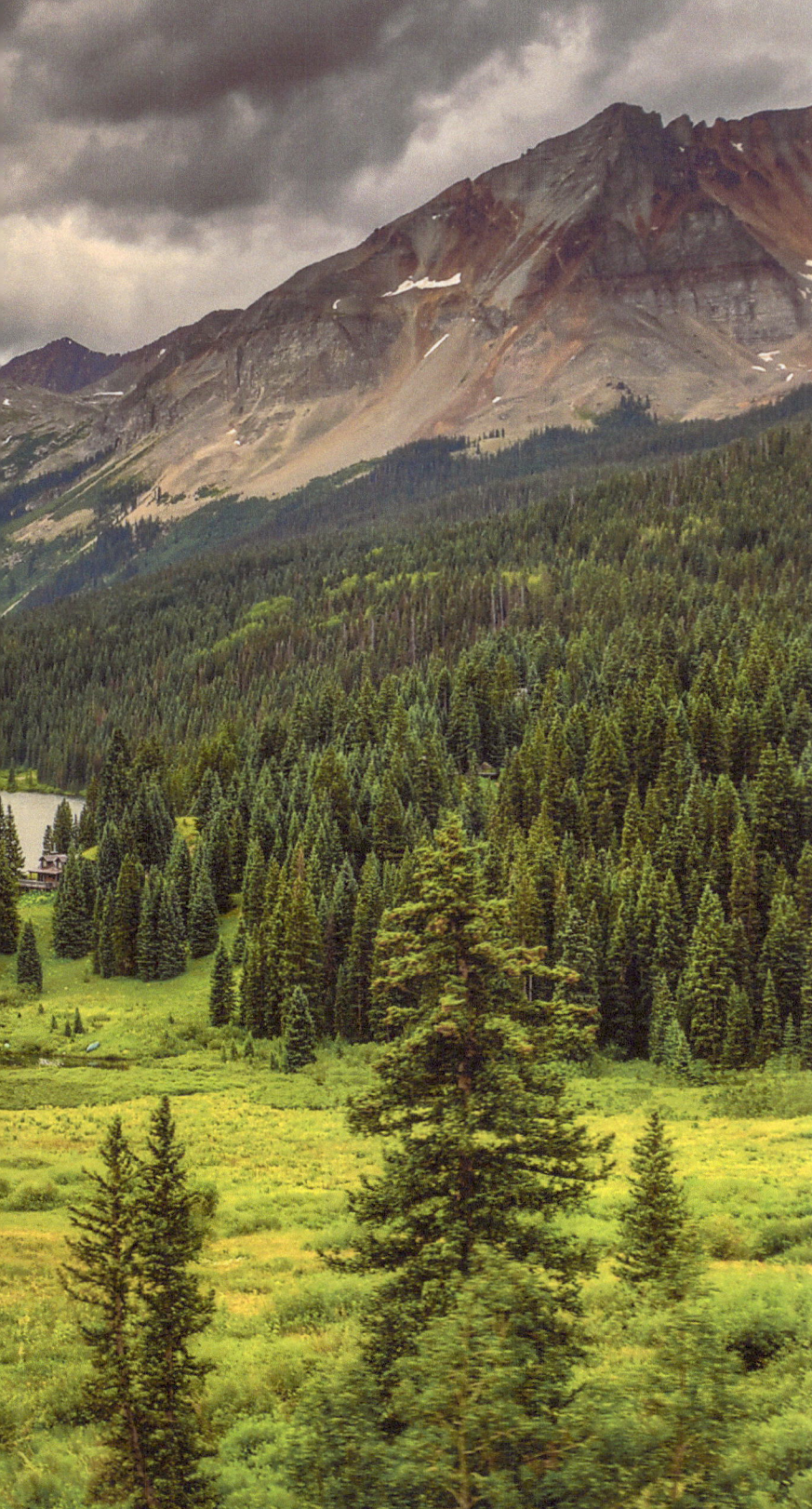

The opening verses found in Genesis 1 are familiar to anyone who has ever read the Bible or attended church or Sunday school.

They chronicle the creation of the earth and all that is in it. Many people could recite some, if not all, of these verses, yet I wonder how many people notice that during each of the first five days of creation the Bible repeats a common phrase—*"and God saw that it was good."* In the New International Version Bible, this phrase is repeated six times in verses 3–24. If God saw that something was good, isn't it fitting that we recognize this as well? Too often we go through the busyness of life and fail to see all the good, all the beauty that surrounds us. How many times have we driven the same road or walked the same path only to suddenly see something we had never noticed before? That tree with the crooked trunk; that flower garden bloom-

TROUT LAKE,
TELLURIDE, COLORADO

| 3

ing with brilliant colors; that patch of cattails that wave back and forth in the summer breezes? What other things have we missed?

In the years since discovering my passion for photography, I have begun to see the beauty that surrounds me with new eyes. I find myself looking at a plowed field differently than I did before. I see the chiseled lines that follow the contour of the earth instead of a black mess waiting for the rains to fall. I view the sunset through the eyes of a painter looking for just the right color palette. I see insects as the amazing creatures they are instead of the menace they once seemed to be. Each one of us has the ability to see things through God's eyes. When we focus on those things that are good, those things that are beautiful, those things that are mysterious, life takes on a whole new meaning. We can see beauty where none existed before, and when we find it, joy will follow suit. Looking for the beauty around us can change our lives, but we must be intentional for change to occur. When we set our minds on the task of seeking beauty in the ashes, we will find it. It's there . . . we just need to look for it.

Like a photographer, God wants all of us to develop an appreciative eye for his creation. He had us in mind when He created the universe, and all of creation is here for us. We, who deserve nothing, have been given everything. He wants us to see beauty in those places where, in our limited sight, no beauty existed before. When we begin to do this, we begin to see the world as God sees the world—for all the good that it is. ଓ

2

New Beginnings

"Satisfy us in the morning with your unfailing love, that we may sing for joy and be glad all our days."

PSALM 90:14 (NIV)

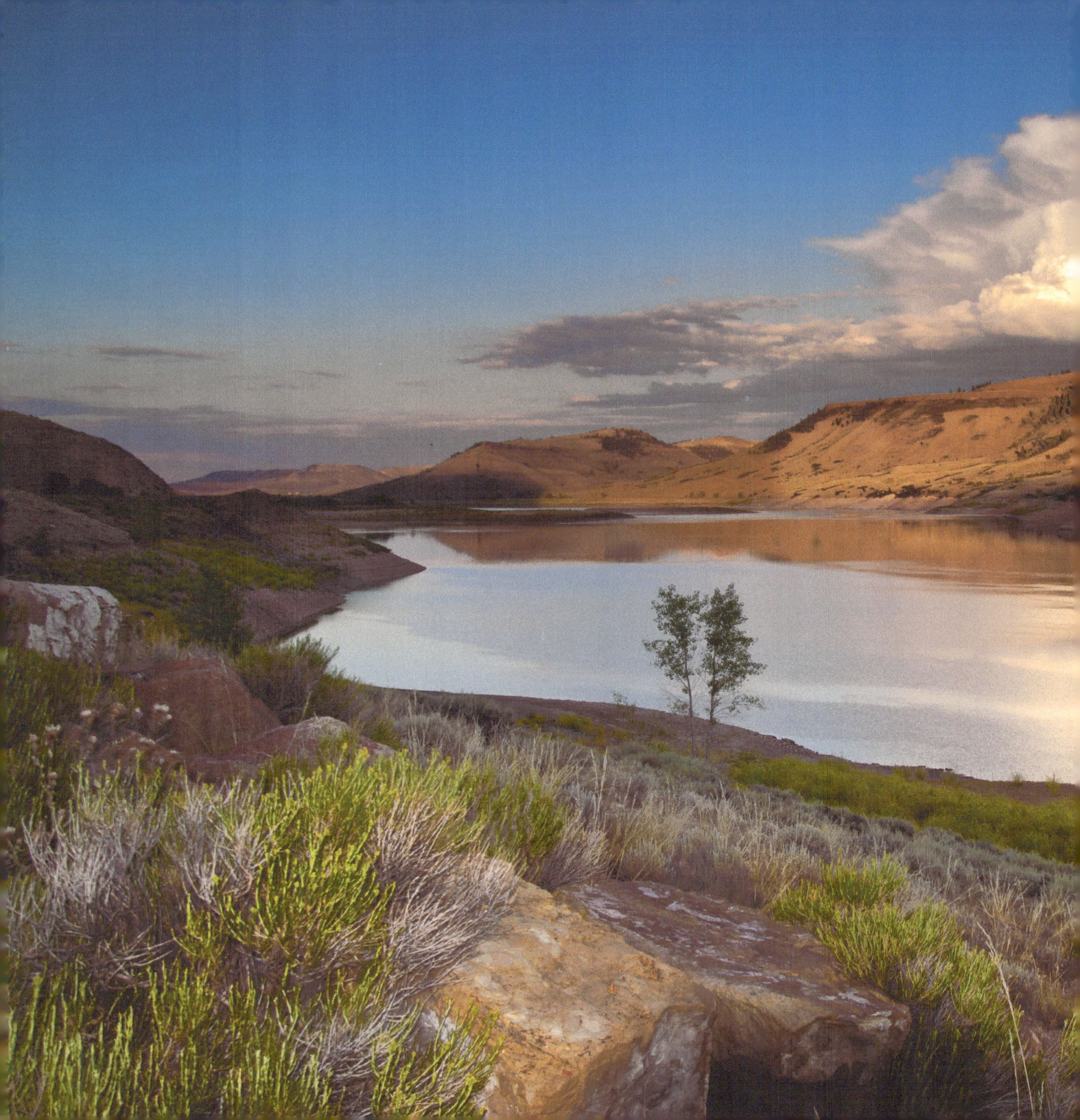

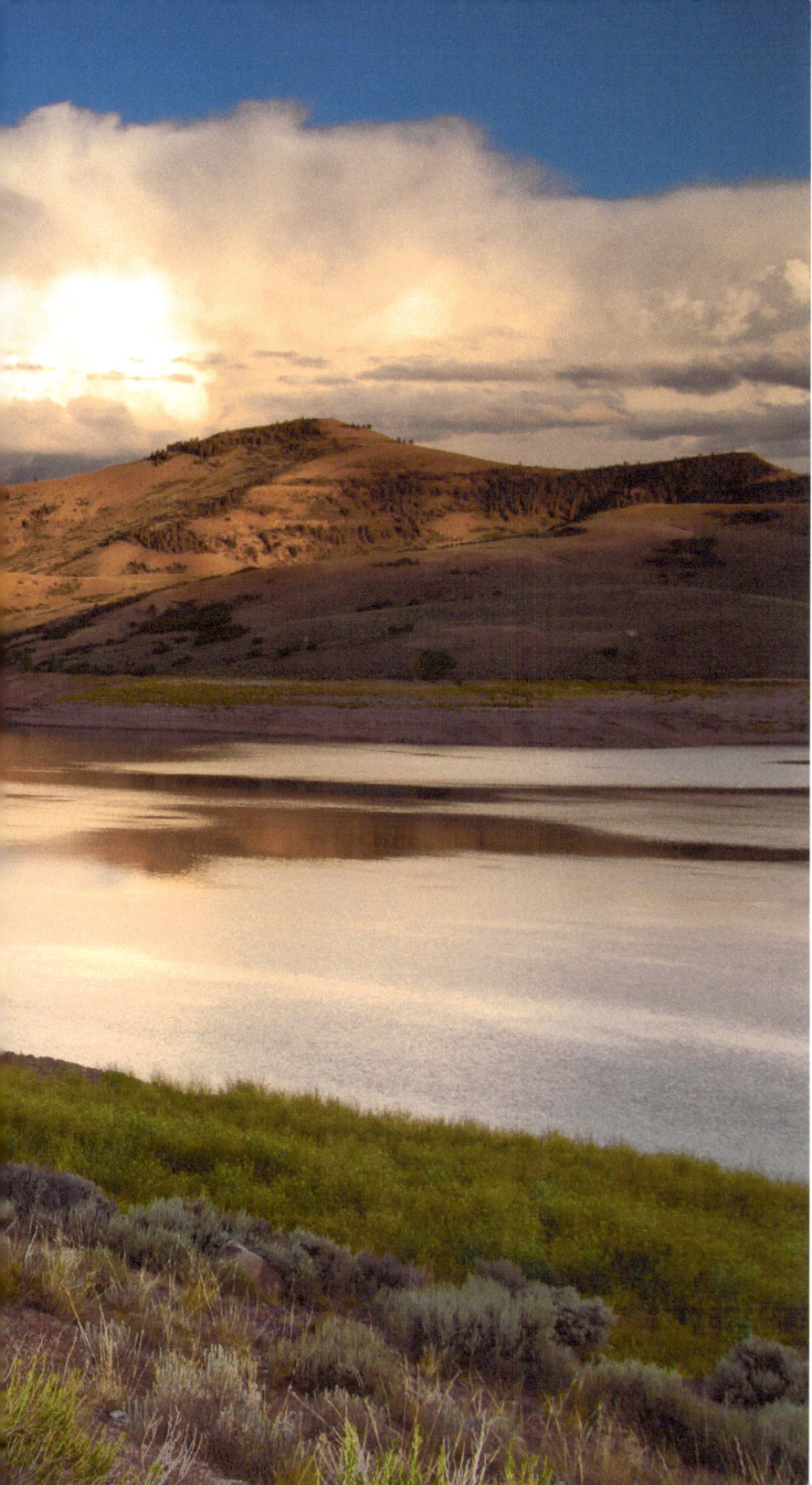

Someone once said, "Each day is a new beginning, a chance to start over again."

I strongly believe in the power of these words. We do not have to live our lives today the same way we did the day before. There is no "rewind" button that takes us back to the events from the day before, nor are we like Phil in the movie *Groundhog Day* where he relives the same day over and over and over again. *Au contraire, mon ami.* We have the option to start anew each and every day.

A few months ago I went through a very low period in my life. I felt like a terrible wrong had been done to me, and I nurtured that hurt and pain for so long that it began to swallow me. The rejection I felt was affecting my attitude, my job, my relationships, my heart . . . everything . . . in a very negative way. I was not enjoying life, and I definitely was not happy. I knew I needed things to change, but I didn't know how to go about it.

Then it happened. My life finally turned a corner—not because of anything I did, but because the God I love loves ME and wants me to live a more

BLUE MESA RESERVOIR, GUNNISON COUNTY, COLORADO

abundant life. I remember it clearly. It was a Wednesday. I woke up angry that I had to face yet another disappointing day. As I sat on the bed and looked out the window, it happened. I clearly heard the voice of God telling me to look for something in which I could find joy and be grateful. So, I took God's advice. And you know what? He was right! I have so much to be joyful for. It didn't make sense for me to focus only on that one negative thing. My life had so much more for which I could be grateful. I just needed that small nudge to help me see it.

That day I became new again. That small shift in my mind's focus made all the difference in my little corner of the world. No, not every day is easy, and yes, I still find myself being negative at times, but I don't stay there. I remind myself to look up, to look around! I find joy in the simple things. These things are gifts from God. As I focus on them, I find my attitude is where it needs to be.

It has become my life's mission to find joy in everything I do—to find the positive instead of focusing on the negative. When God tells me to do something, I must listen and obey.

All of us must focus more on the gifts God has given us and less on our circumstances or the faults of others. It is then, and only then, that we find the joy David talks about in the Psalms. With an attitude of gratitude, the beauty of God's hand will reveal itself all the days of our lives. ∽

3

Lest the Rocks Cry Out

"When he came near the place where the road goes down the Mount of Olives, the whole crowd of disciples began joyfully to praise God in loud voices for all the miracles they had seen: 'Blessed is the king who comes in the name of the Lord! Peace in heaven and glory in the highest!' Some of the Pharisees in the crowd said to Jesus, 'Teacher, rebuke your disciples!' 'I tell you,' he replied, 'if they keep quiet, the stones will cry out.'"

LUKE 19:37-40 (NIV)

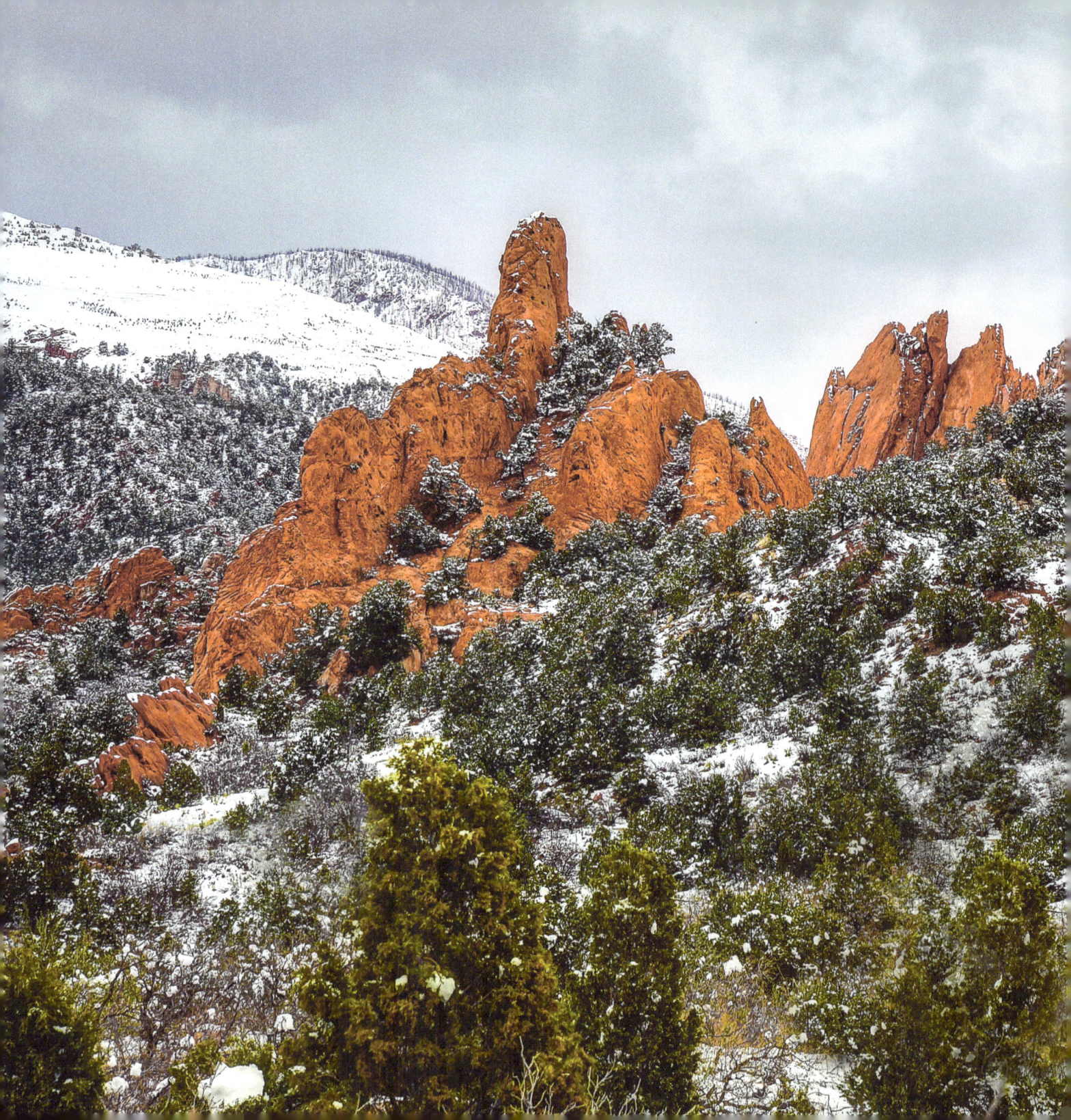

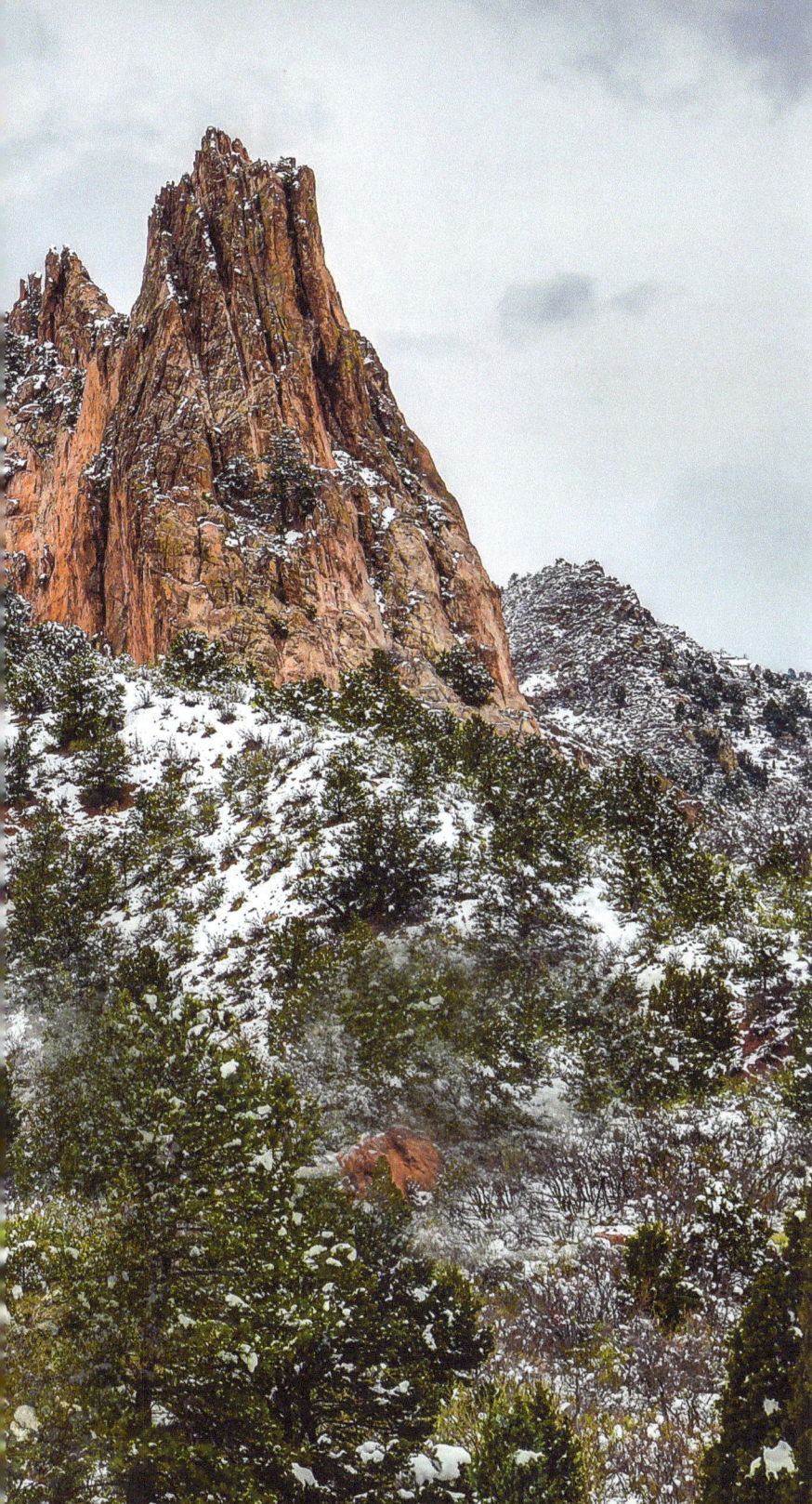

Webster defines the word miracle as "an unusual or wonderful event that is believed to be caused by the power of God."

When Jesus walked the face of the Earth two thousand years ago, his followers witnessed countless numbers of miracles—those events that could only be attributed to the power of God.

In Luke 19 we read about Jesus' entry into the city of Jerusalem. Prior to his arrival, he sent two of his disciples to fetch a colt that had not yet been ridden that was tied at the gate. They were instructed to tell those who asked what they were doing that *"The Lord needs it."* His powerful presence was so commanding and compelling that those who had witnessed the miracles could not be silenced. They knew from whom the miracles had come. No, they could not be silenced. Instead they sang praises to God. Their praise placed their hope, their future, their security, their salvation in Jesus. They were honoring Jesus as

GARDEN OF THE GODS, COLORADO SPRINGS, COLORADO

God, the Messiah who had come to deliver them.

The Pharisees, however, knew a threat when they saw one. They knew that Jesus of Nazareth was threatening their earthly authority, so they demanded that he control his followers by silencing them. In his infinite wisdom, however, Jesus replied, *"If they keep quiet, the rocks will cry out."* The very earth, created by God the Father, would stand in the gap and sing the praises due our Lord and Savior if those who knew him would not.

Is it possible that now, two thousand years later, the rocks would still cry out? YES! Just look around you. They cry out every moment of every day. God's beauty is everywhere, and it screams volumes of praises. No, we cannot audibly hear the rocks cry out, but sometimes silence says it all. Those who SEE the glory of God through the incredible beauty of his handiwork can HEAR the praises. I believe the words Jesus spoke two thousand years ago still hold true today. God inhabits the praises of His people. If we refuse to sing His praises, then like Jesus declared, the rocks will. We owe it to God to give Him the praise He is due. Sing His praises. Shout them to the heavens. Don't let the rocks cry out in your stead. ∽

4

Let the Rivers Clap

"Let the rivers clap their hands, let the mountains sing together for joy."

PSALM 98:8 (NIV)

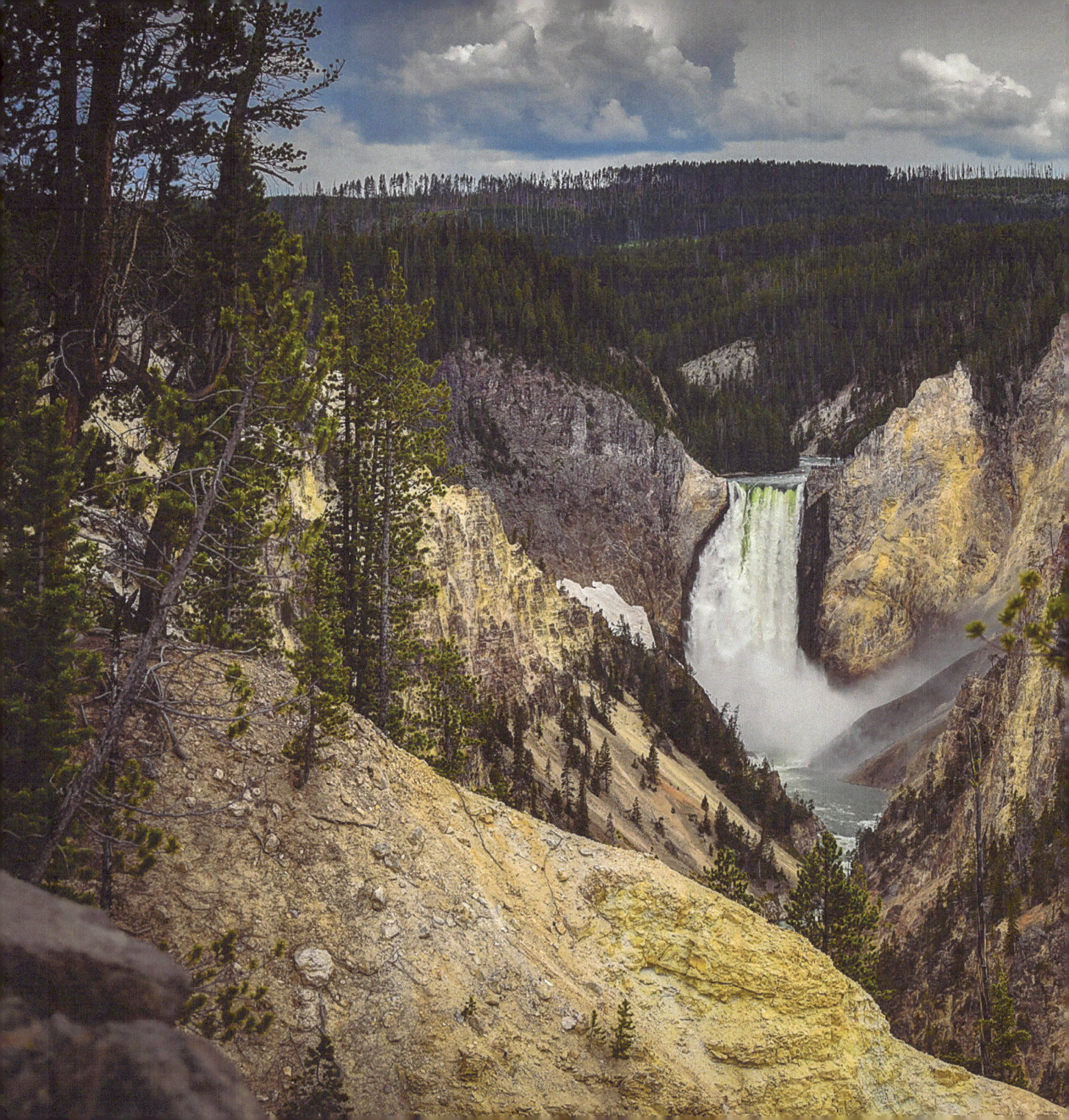

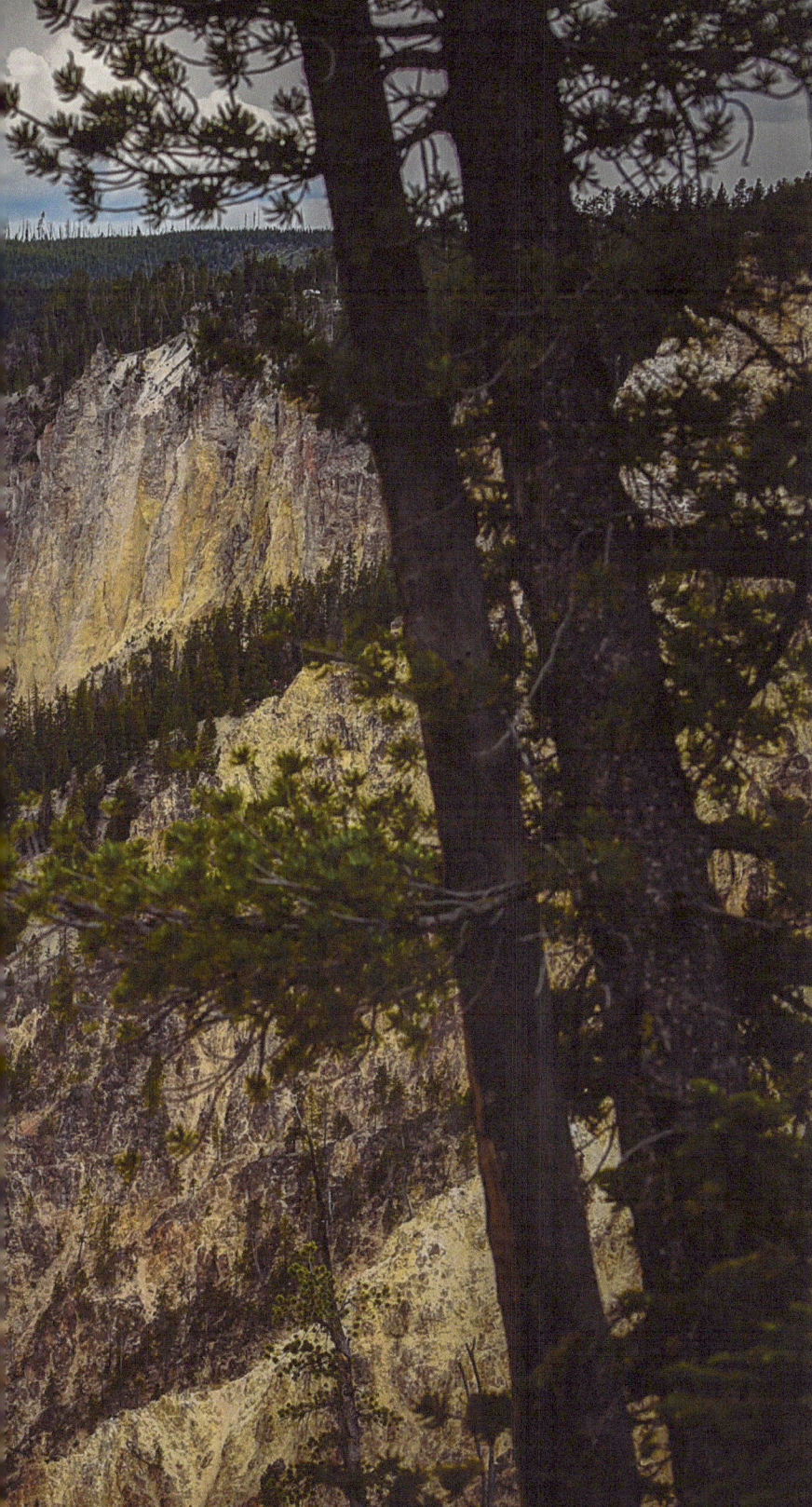

Since becoming a photographer, I have found myself doing things I wouldn't normally do.

I get excited when I see an insect instead of cringing at the sight of the strange creature. I spend time looking around me instead of hurrying to get to my final destination. I get up early to sit out in the cold in the hopes of witnessing a delicate deer head back to her resting grounds. I've even climbed trees to get above the sight lines of animals out in the forest. It is during these moments that I feel especially close to God.

When I am out in nature, I often stop, look around, and listen. I think about the wonders of our world. I chuckle at the little squirrel puttering around searching for nuts to store for the long, cold winter. I marvel at a hawk soaring effortlessly above the meadow as its eyes scan the ground for its next meal. I shiver in the cool breeze that rustles the leaves of the trees into an amazing chorus of sound. I watch in wonder at a doe and two yearlings as they timidly step out into the

LOWER FALLS, YELLOWSTONE NATIONAL PARK, WYOMING

dwindling sunshine. I take time to focus on the little gifts God has given us.

The Psalms are filled with references to finding joy in nature. David knew the maker of the universe, and he continually cried out in praise to the maker of that universe. All of nature sings praise to the maker. If the rivers clap their hands, and the mountains sing together for joy, how much more should we? After all, we are the very children of that maker.

As we go through each day, it is essential to stop, look, and listen. We need to look for those little things in which to rejoice. If not for those small things, it would be easy to get swallowed up in all the other things that are pressing in against us. Our lives are filled with "stuff" that seeks to steal our joy. We have beds to make, mouths to feed, kids to corral, bills to pay, lawns to mow, spouses to please, jobs to do, meetings to attend, and on and on it goes. There seems to be a never-ending list of demands, all quarreling for our time and attention. It is no wonder people get so caught up in the busyness of life that they fail to see the beauty around them. What a tragedy it would be to reach the end of our lives on Earth only to discover how much of it we really missed.

It's not always easy to stop and just sit. If we see things that need to be done, we think we need to do them. However, if we wish to live a full life, we must stop and look around. When we take time to praise God for the little things, our lives become much richer. ␣

5

Lessons From a Darkroom

"Not only that, but we rejoice in our sufferings, knowing that suffering produces endurance, and endurance produces character, and character produces hope, and hope does not put us to shame, because God's love has been poured into our hearts through the Holy Spirit who has been given to us."

ROMANS 5:3–5 (ESV)

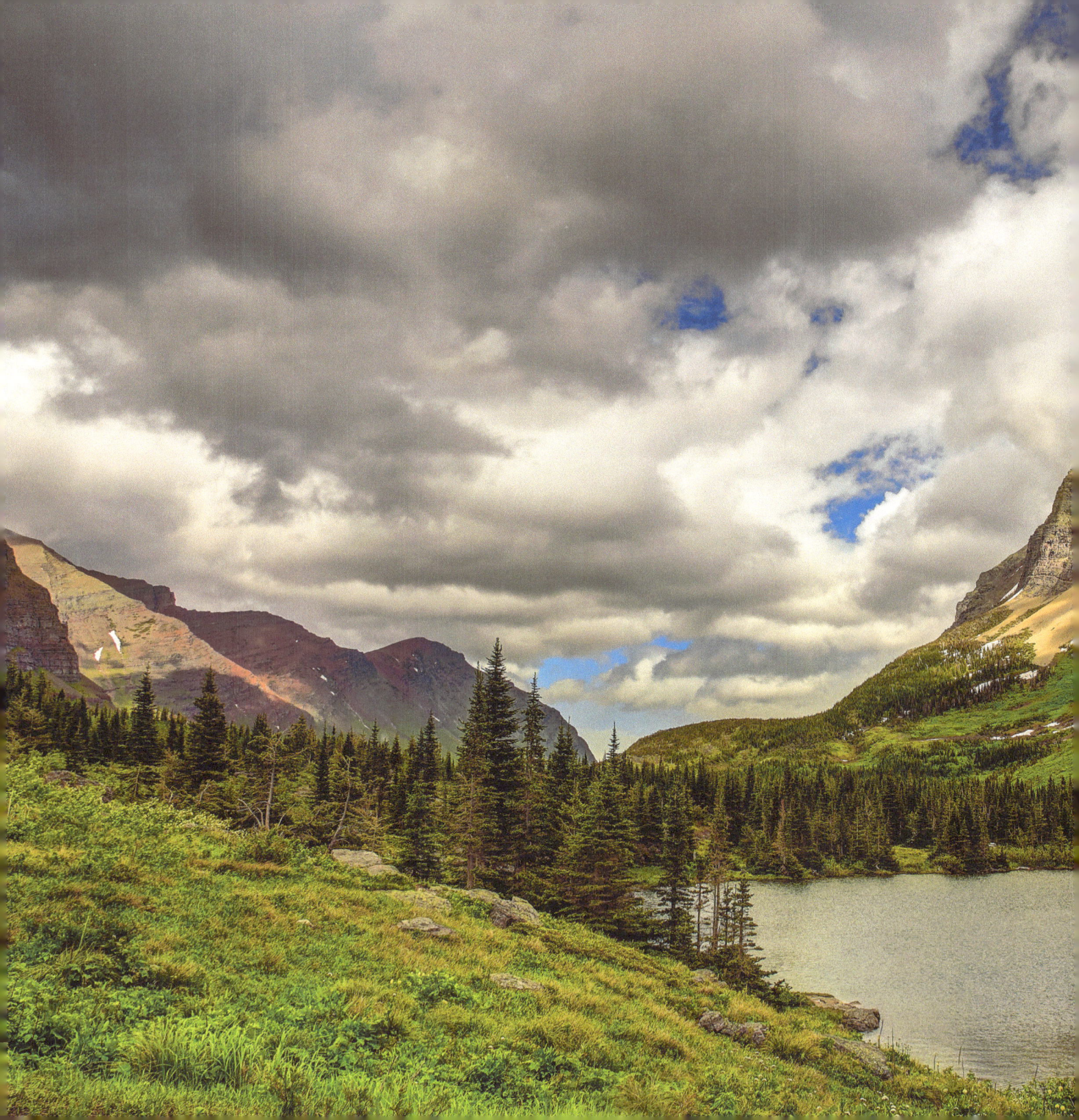

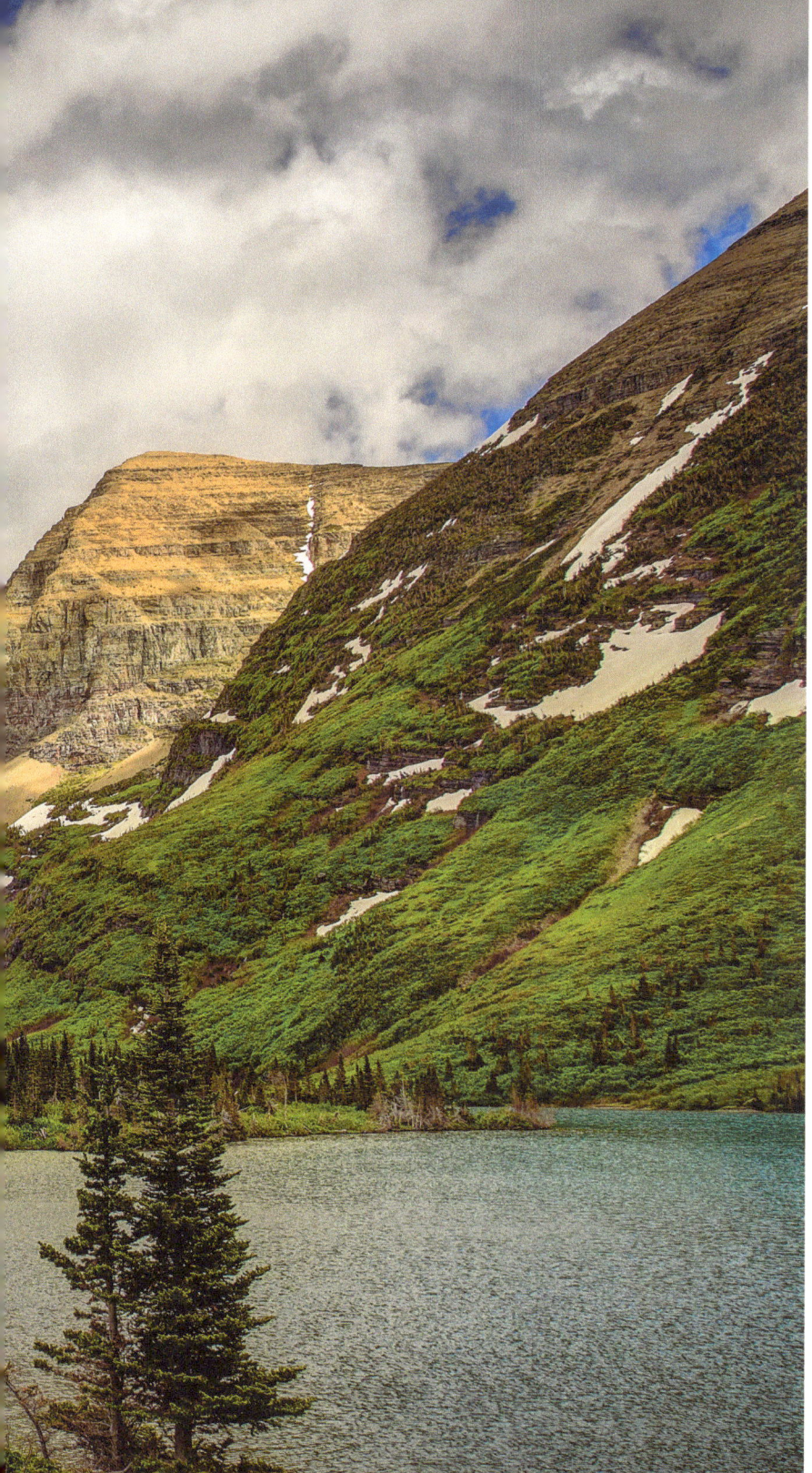

I have never had the experience of working in a darkroom where photos were developed using the "old-school" methods my father used.

Using only the illumination of a red light, the film was transferred onto special photo paper, which was then dipped in different trays holding chemical solutions. As the photo paper was moved from tray to tray, the image would begin to emerge. The process took a considerable amount of time and care and seemed mysteriously magical.

There was no magic involved though—only science. Since photo paper reacts to light, camera film needed to be produced in a room that was completely dark. It was hard for the photographer to see what he was doing in complete darkness, though, so darkrooms used red lighting to control light levels. The light-sensitive photo paper did not react to the red light, so it would not become

HIDDEN LAKE, BANFF NATIONAL PARK, ALBERTA, CANADA

overexposed and ruined during the developing process.

While I've never experienced working in a darkroom firsthand, I know enough about old-school photo processing to know that darkroom intruders were the enemy. Anyone who opened the darkroom door during development of the film put the entire processing at risk. If too much light flooded into the darkroom during processing, an entire batch of painstakingly crafted film would be ruined.

Like film, God allows darkrooms to develop us. When we experience the darkness of financial reversal, job loss, sickness, disappointment, loneliness, death, and countless other trials, we need to look at things as though we are in a darkroom. Christ's blood is the red light that covers us and protects us from the light waves of the enemy. Like photographers, we must wait patiently inside the darkroom and watch as God takes time and care to develop the picture of our lives—a picture that He has taken great care in planning. We mustn't rush through any of the stages. Only when the process is complete will we be fully developed. We will only be ready for "print" when we allow His image to emerge through us. ଔ

6

The Wisdom Behind the V

"Two are better than one, because they have a good reward for their toil. For if they fall, one will lift up his fellow. But woe to him who is alone when he falls and has not another to lift him up! Again, if two lie together, they keep warm, but how can one keep warm alone? And though a man might prevail against one who is alone, two will withstand him—a threefold cord is not quickly broken."

ECCLESIASTES 4:9–12 (ESV)

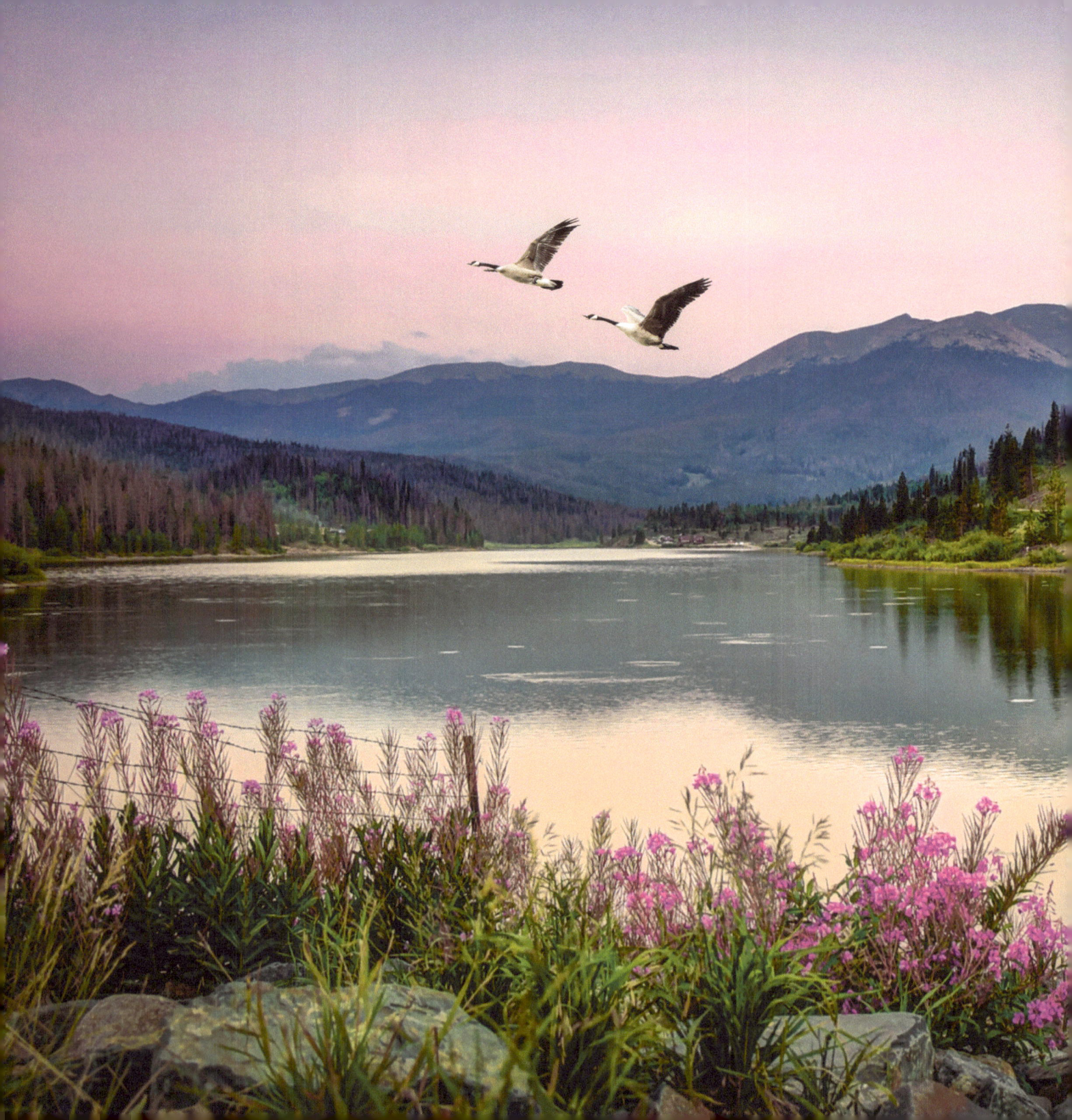

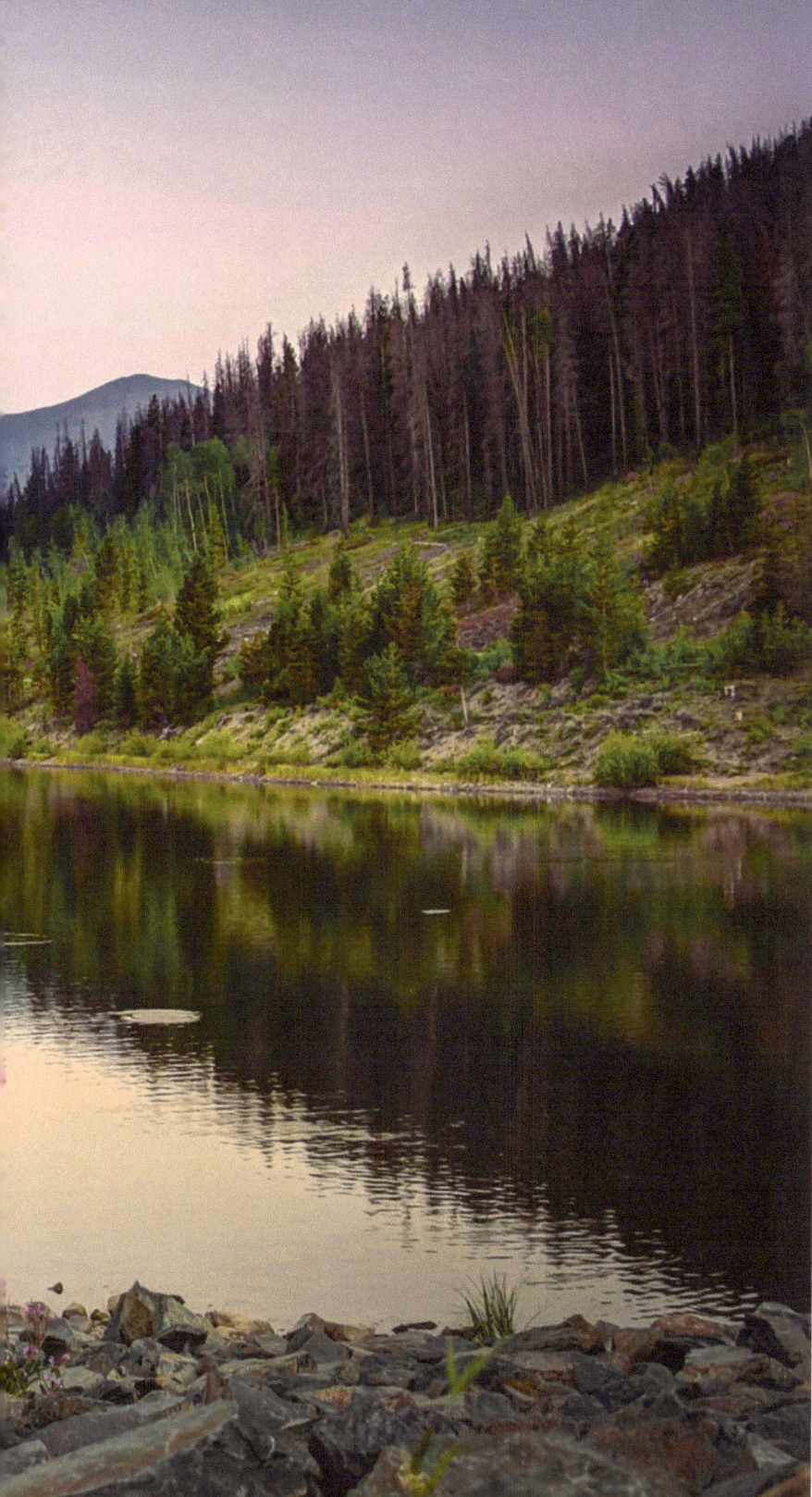

Have you ever watched a flock of geese flying through the air?

Flying in V-formation, their flight plan is simple. Amazing, yet simple. They work together to get from one point to another. One cannot view a flock of geese without staring in amazement at the wonder of nature and the intelligence of these big-bodied birds. We can learn a lot from geese.

When geese fly in formation, the leader does the hardest work. It is his job to carve a path through the air. When he flaps his wings, he creates an "up wash"—the downward push of air as the body cuts through the air. The birds behind use the up wash to their own benefit. By putting their wingtips in the up wash, they get a free ride of sorts. Their task is made easier by the efforts of the bird ahead. The birds save energy by using the good air from the bird in front. When the lead bird tires, he takes his place further back in the flock, and a different bird takes the lead. They share the work-load so that each member of the flock takes his turn. But it doesn't stop there.

CANADIAN GEESE IN FLIGHT, NORTHERN COLORADO

Not only do the geese share the workload, but the ones behind honk "words" of encouragement to those ahead.

If the human race took lessons from the geese, we could learn a few things. We all need to do our fair share of the work and not simply get by on the "up wash" of those who lead. We need to take the lead once in awhile and let those who lead take a rest. Sometimes we need to do what is difficult, but if we have supporters to encourage us along the way, we are more likely to be successful.

In Ecclesiastes, we are reminded that *"two are better than one."* God is telling us to depend on one another, to encourage one another, to work with one another. If man were meant to do it alone, God would not have created Eve, Adam's helpmate. He knew that two are better than one, so the creator of the universe made it possible for Adam to have a helper, an encourager.

However, Ecclesiastes 4:12 takes this concept one step further. It says,". . . *a threefold cord is not easily broken."* But whom does this third strand represent? Didn't the previous verses only mention two? Why, all of a sudden, are there three? God is telling us to not only lean on one another, but to also include HIM as well. When we have earthly helpers, leaders, and encouragers, we can accomplish much, but by adding God to the mix, we can do great things.

The geese know about this truth. Let's follow their lead. The next time you hear the chorus of a flock of geese, take time to look up. Look up, enjoy the view, think about the wisdom behind the V, and let your heart swell with joy at the wonder of it all. ॐ

7

Just Go Fishing

"Therefore do not worry about tomorrow, for tomorrow will worry about itself. Each day has enough trouble of its own."

MATTHEW 6:34 (NIV)

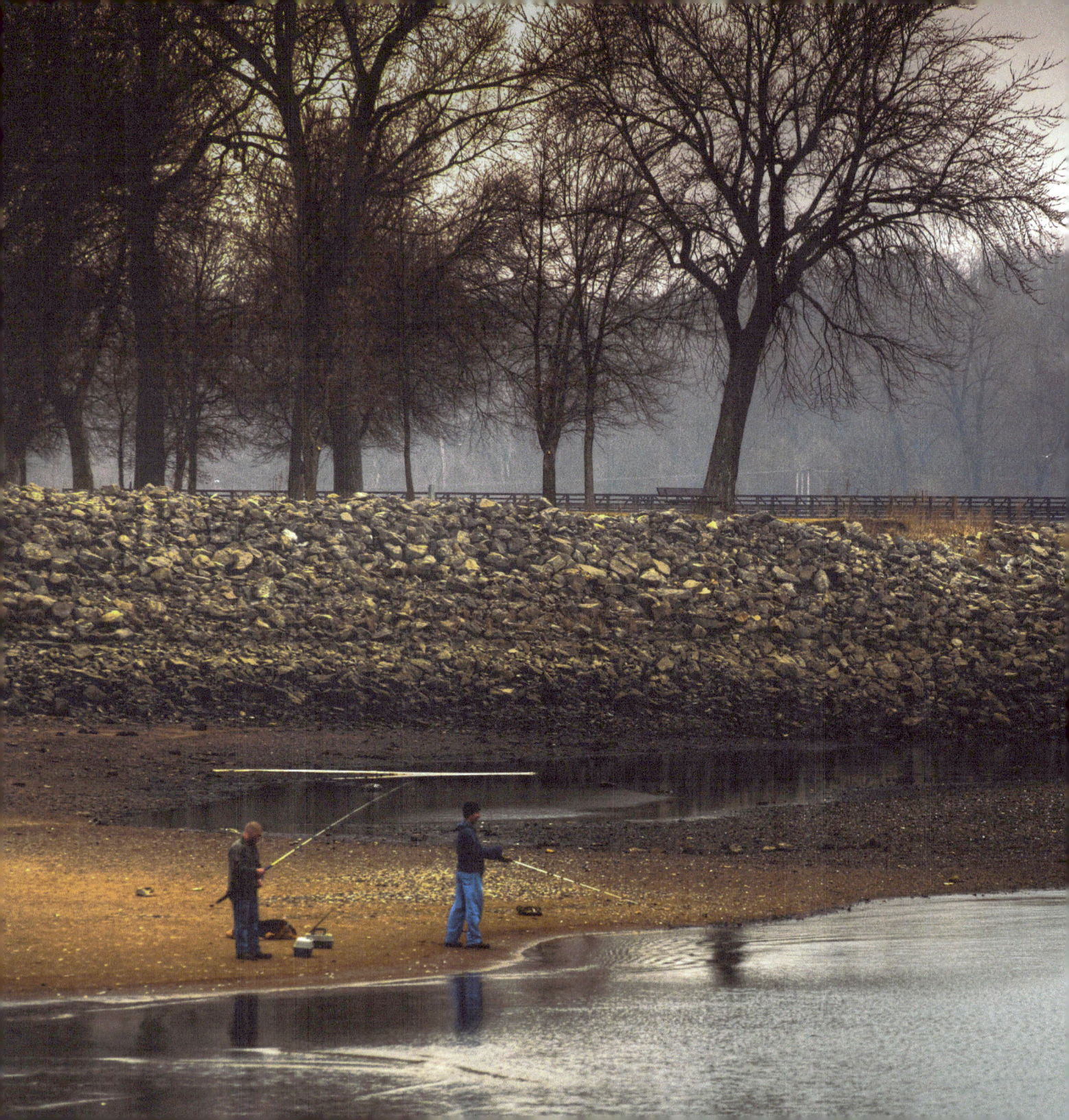

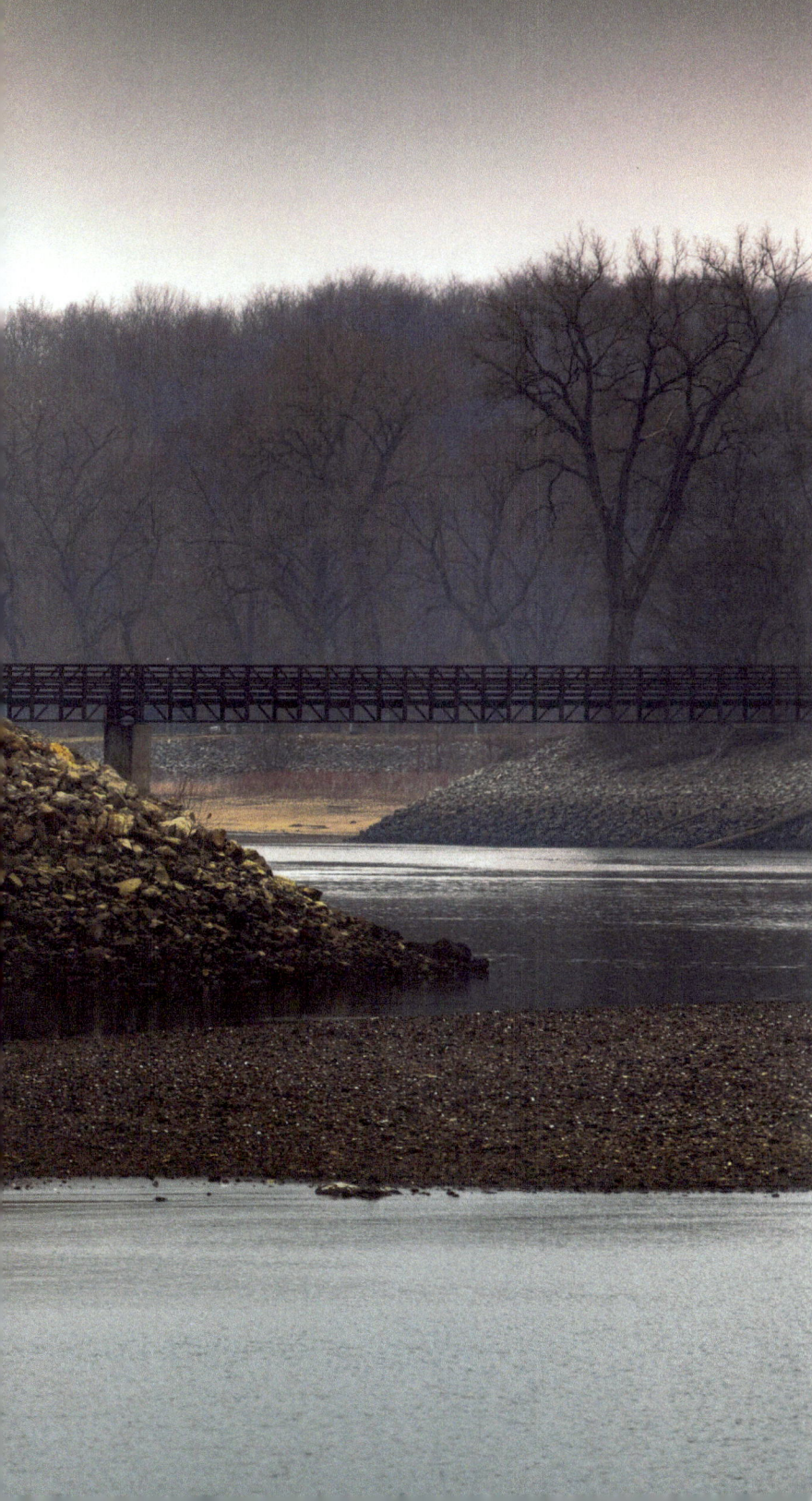

Sometimes the things that happen in our lives get in the way of living. Wait! Say that again?

". . . the things that happen in our lives get in the way of living"? Yes, life sometimes gets in the way of life. We get so wrapped up in the stuff that clogs our lives that we forget what Jesus told his disciples in John 10:10: *"The thief does not come except to steal, and to kill, and to destroy. I have come that they may have life, and that they may have it more abundantly"* (NKJV). While the original Bible teachings of this verse refer to those who entered the priesthood for the sole purpose of reaping the benefits of the church, I believe we can apply this in a different way in our contemporary world. In today's world, the "thief" can be translated to those things that steal our joy and keep us from seeing and receiving the blessings of God: things that demand our time and steal our joy. The quest for more steals our joy. Even doing good for others, including the church, can steal our joy. Anything that takes our

FISHING ON THE DES MOINES RIVER, RED ROCK DAM, PELLA, IOWA

| 27

eyes off of Jesus and shifts our sight to earthly things is a thief that steals the joy Christ wants for us.

However, those aren't the only thieves in our lives. Worry is a thief. Anxiety is a thief. Fear is a thief. These things also steal our joy. Too often we spend time and energy worrying about the things we cannot change; the things that are beyond our control. In Matthew 6:26 (ESV) God reminds us not to worry. *"Behold the birds of the air, for they neither sow nor reap nor gather into barns; yet your heavenly Father feeds them. Are you not of more value than they? Which of you by worrying can add one hour to his life?"* In Philippians 4:6 (NIV) we read, *"Do not be anxious about anything, but in every situation, by prayer and petition, with thanksgiving, present your requests to God."* And 1 Peter 5:7 (NIV) says, *"Cast all your anxiety on Him because He cares for you."* God promises that if we keep our eyes on Him and set our feet on the path down which He leads, He will take care of us. He doesn't promise us a life without trials, but He provides a haven in which we can rest when the trials come.

A.W. Tozer once said, "Sometimes when we get overwhelmed we forget how big God is." It is easy to get overwhelmed and focus only on the trial directly in front of us. But that is contrary to what God wants us to do. Instead He asks that we set our sights on Him always. All of us must take this truth to heart. We must let go of our worries and anxieties, and look to our big God to help us through each day, regardless of the trials we are facing. Matthew 6:34 (NIV) tells us, *"do not worry about tomorrow, for tomorrow will worry about itself. Each day has enough trouble of its own."*

When we find ourselves anxious, worried, or just plain too busy, we need to take time to reflect on God's promises. We need to find something to do that connects us to the creator. Nothing does that better than looking to nature; take a hike, go fishing, or sit in the back yard and watch the birds. If God takes care of the birds, He'll certainly take care of us. Letting go of our worries is not easy to do, but God can handle it. We can lean on Him and cling to His promises. He will never leave us nor forsake us. ❧

8

On Wings Like Eagles

"The Lord is the everlasting God, the Creator of the ends of the earth. He will not grow tired or weary, and his understanding no one can fathom. He gives strength to the weary and increases the power of the weak. Even youths grow tired and weary, and young men stumble and fall; but those who hope in the Lord will renew their strength. They will soar on wings like eagles; they will run and not grow weary, they will walk and not be faint."

ISAIAH 40:28–31 (NIV)

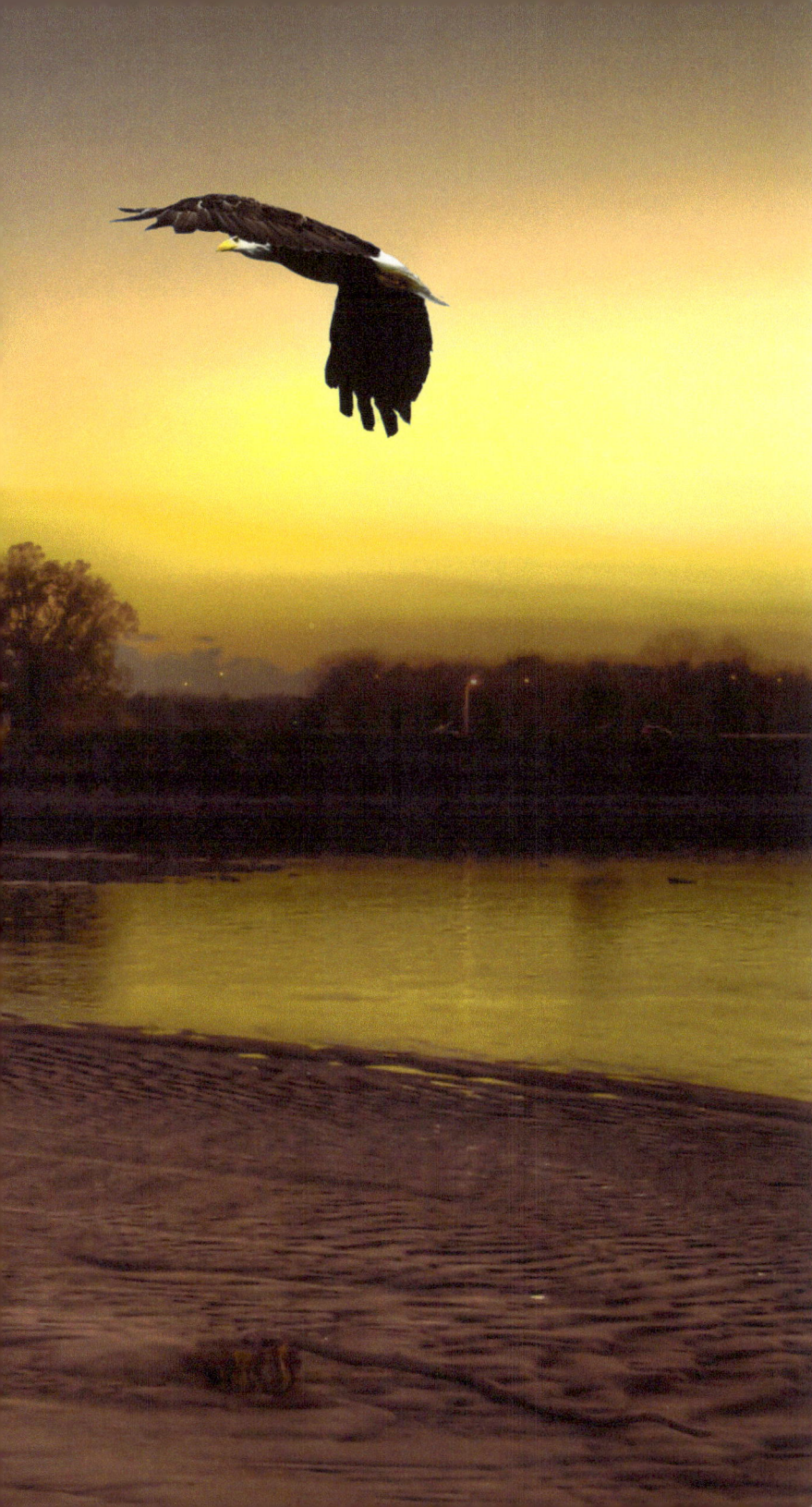

Have you ever been weary?

The kind of weary that makes even the simplest of tasks nearly impossible to accomplish? Webster defines this kind of weary as "exhausted in strength, endurance, vigor, or freshness." We have all had times when it seemed our strength to carry on was totally gone. Everything we had in us was spent, and we had nothing left to give. It seemed like we had waited and waited upon the Lord, begged Him to hear our cry, to answer our prayers, to lift us out of the pit, but to no avail. He was silent. We've all been there. But God has promised never to leave us. The Bible is filled with promise after promise that He is with us, that He cares for us.

"It is the Lord who goes before you. He will be with you; he will not leave you or forsake you. Do not fear or be dismayed." Deuteronomy 31:8 (NAS)

"Be strong and courageous. Do not fear or be in dread of them, for it is the Lord your God who goes with you. He will not leave you or forsake you." Deuteronomy 31:6 (ESV)

"Have I not commanded you? Be strong and courageous. Do not be fright-

BRIDGE STREET BRIDGE
OVER THE DES MOINES RIVER,
OTTUMWA, IOWA

ened, and do not be dismayed, for the Lord your God is with you wherever you go." Joshua 1:9 (ESV)

"Cast all your anxieties on him, because he cares for you." 1 Peter 5:7 (NIV)

"Fear not, for I am with you: be not dismayed, for I am your God; I will strengthen you, I will help you, I will uphold you with my righteous right hand. Behold, all who are incensed against you shall be put to shame and confounded; those who strive against you shall be as nothing and shall perish. You shall seek those who contend with you, but you shall not find them; those who war against you shall be as nothing at all. For I, the Lord your God, hold your right hand; it is I who say to you, 'fear not, I am the one who helps you.'" Isaiah 41:10–13 (ESV)

These are the words of the very God who made the heavens and the earth. Over and over again He reminds us that He loves us and will be with us every step of the way. Find rest in these words. Take comfort in knowing that the one who created our amazing world loves us beyond anything we can fathom and will keep His promises to take care of us.

When we find ourselves weary and struggling to go on, we need to wait. Wait, in hope, on the Lord. Wait on the very Lord who promises us that He will never leave us nor forsake us—the very Lord who gives strength to the weary and increases the power of the weak. Wait on the Lord who promises to give renewed strength to those who rest in Him. In God's time, He will lift us up. He will renew our strength. We will soar on wings like eagles. We will run and not grow weary. We will walk and not faint.

In those moments when we have done all we know to do, we must fall to our knees and lift our eyes to the One who speaks these promises. We must trust that His words are true. And we must wait. It is during those times of weakness, when we wait on Him in hope, that we learn what it means to become truly strong in Him. ଔ

9

Joy in the Journey

"Consider it pure joy, my brothers, whenever you face trials of many kinds, because you know that the testing of your faith develops perseverance. Perseverance must finish its work so that you may be mature and complete, not lacking anything."

JAMES 1:2–4 (NIV)

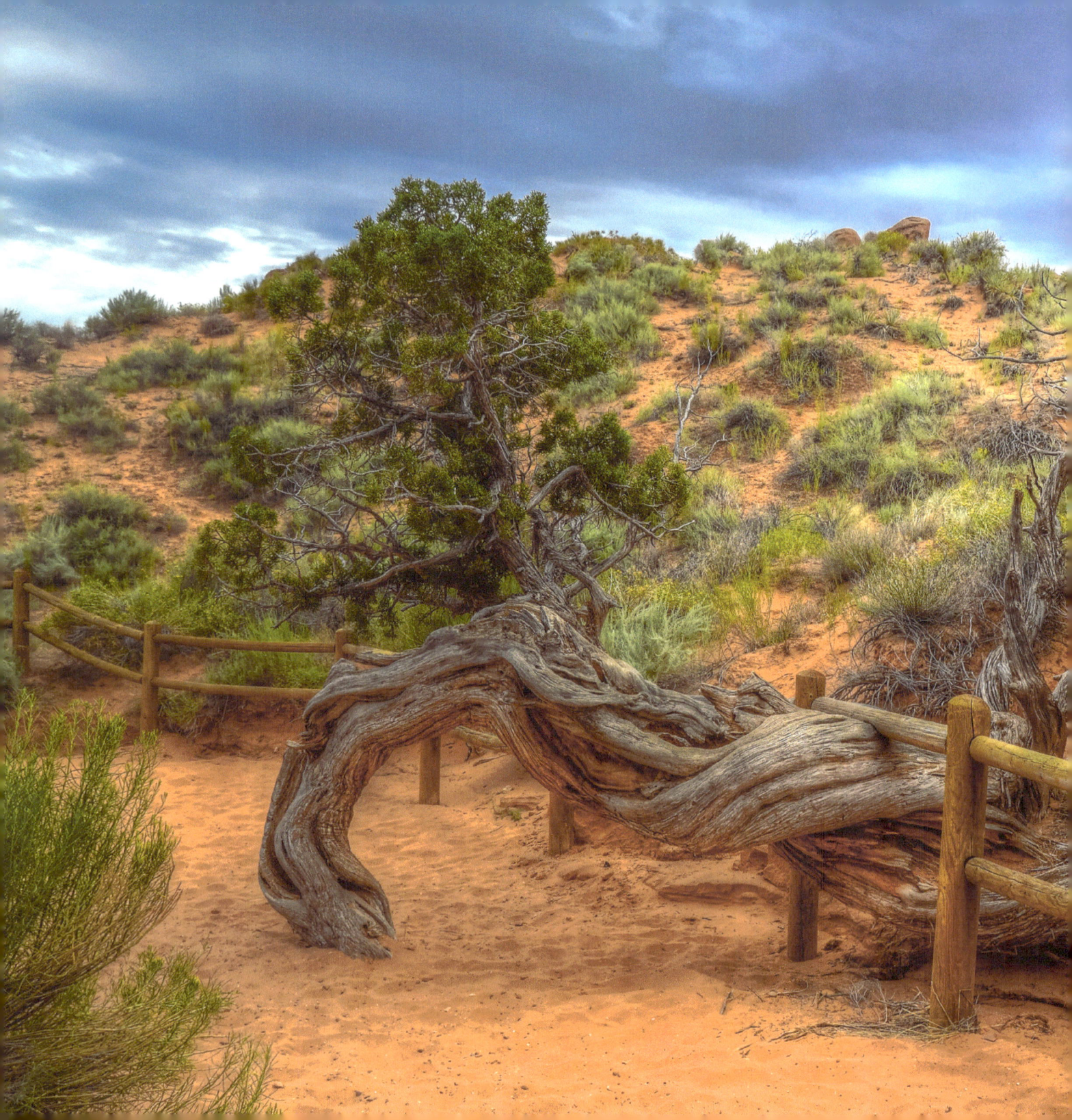

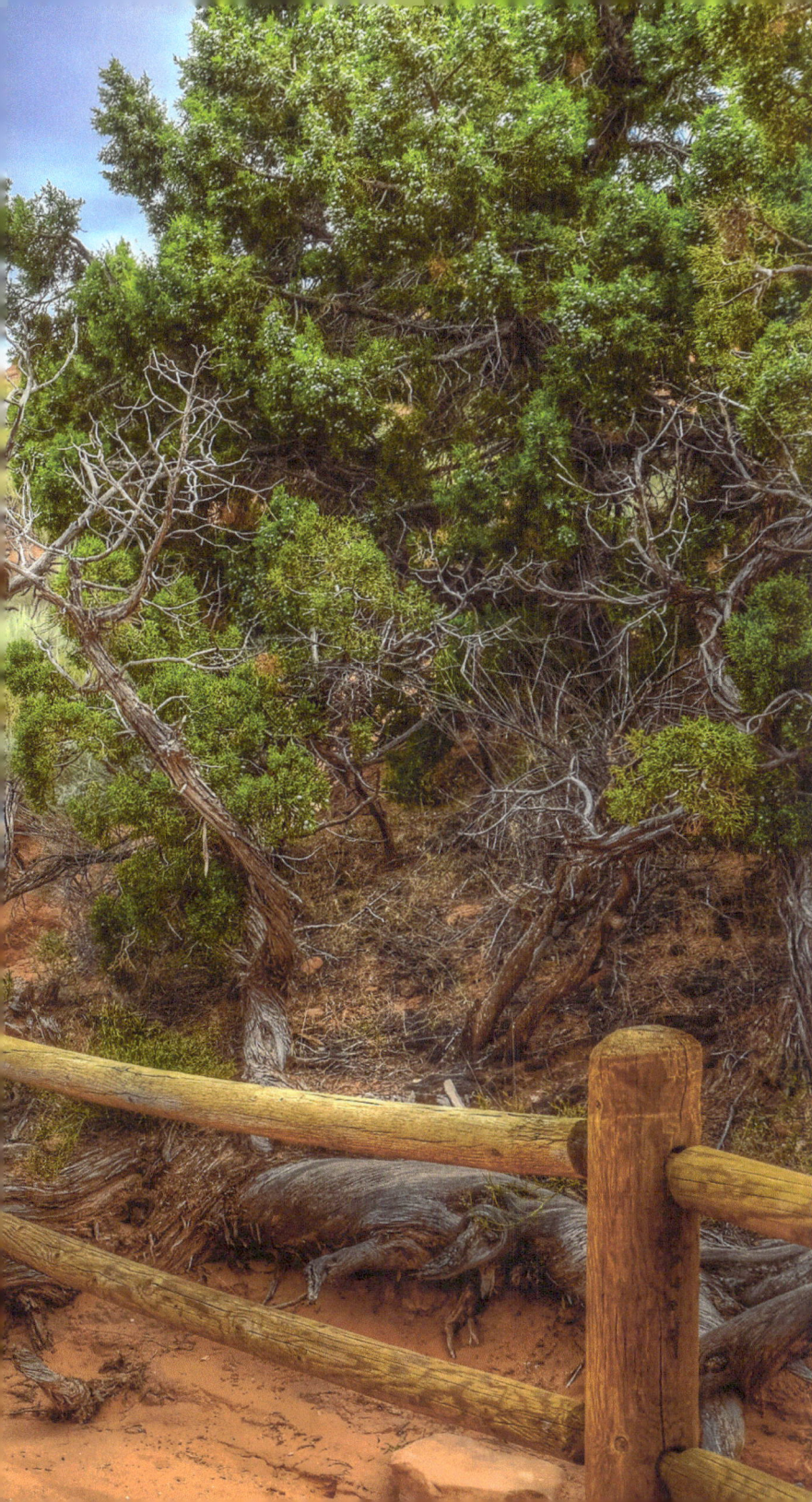

"I love trial, trouble, and hardship!" said no one ever.

Not one of us looks forward to trials, temptations, and hardships. That would be just plain crazy. Yet we are told in James 1 to "consider it pure joy . . . whenever you face trials of many kinds . . ." Joy in hardship? Really? Yes, really. God doesn't want to see any of us, His children, suffer trials. He doesn't look down from heaven and say, "Today I think I am going to make my children suffer." No. That is not how God works. He is not that kind of God. Yet God allows us to go through trials so that we will depend on Him. He wants us to trust in Him at all times, through all things.

In John 16:33 (HCSB), Jesus said, *"You will have suffering in this world."* Notice that He didn't say you *might* have suffering in this world; He said you *will*. It's not a matter of if, it's a matter of when. Trials, however, can be a real test of trust in God. When we meet trials head-on with the right attitude, they serve to prove the quality of faith we have. We must trust in our faith and know that God is the Lord of all. We must trust that He will be with us through it all. And we

TWISTED CEDAR TREE, PATH TO LANDSCAPE ARCH, ARCHES NATIONAL PARK, UTAH must trust that He will give us the strength we need to get through to the end. When we face difficult times, we find ourselves in a state of weakness, a state of dependency on Him. Trials bring us to a point where we have to put our trust in God, thus making our faith in Him stronger.

We will encounter things that twist us and bend us in ways we never deemed possible. But as Christians, we know that when trials come, we can have pure joy. We can have joy because we know that we will overcome and become stronger. We know that the testing of our faith develops perseverance, which will take us through to maturity and completion. The next time you face trials, find the joy in the journey. What you'll find at the end of that journey will be worth it all! ❧

10

Do Like the Aspens

"For just as each of us has one body with many members, and these members do not all have the same function, so in Christ we, though many, form one body, and each member belongs to all the others."

ROMANS 12:4-5 (NIV)

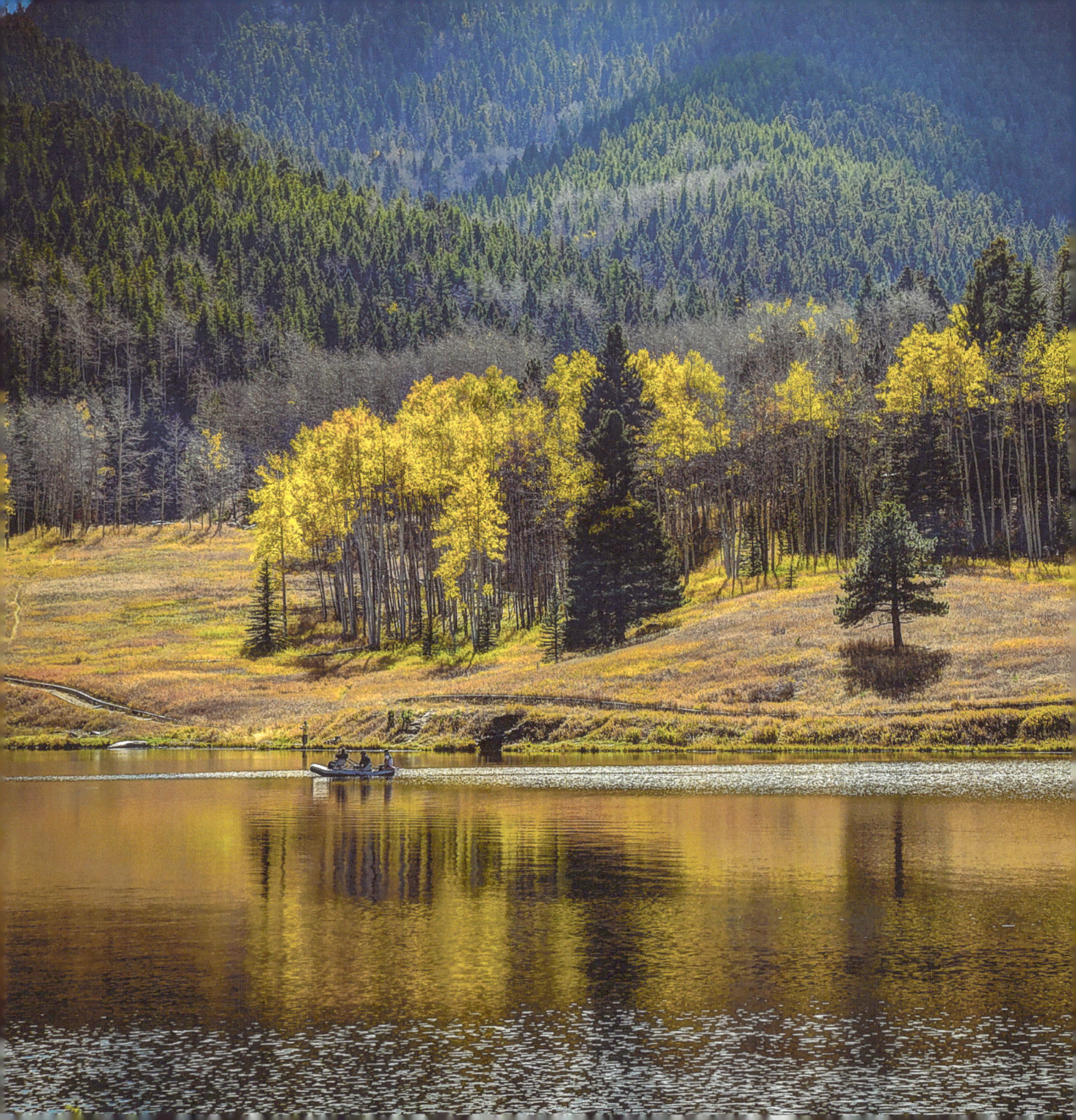

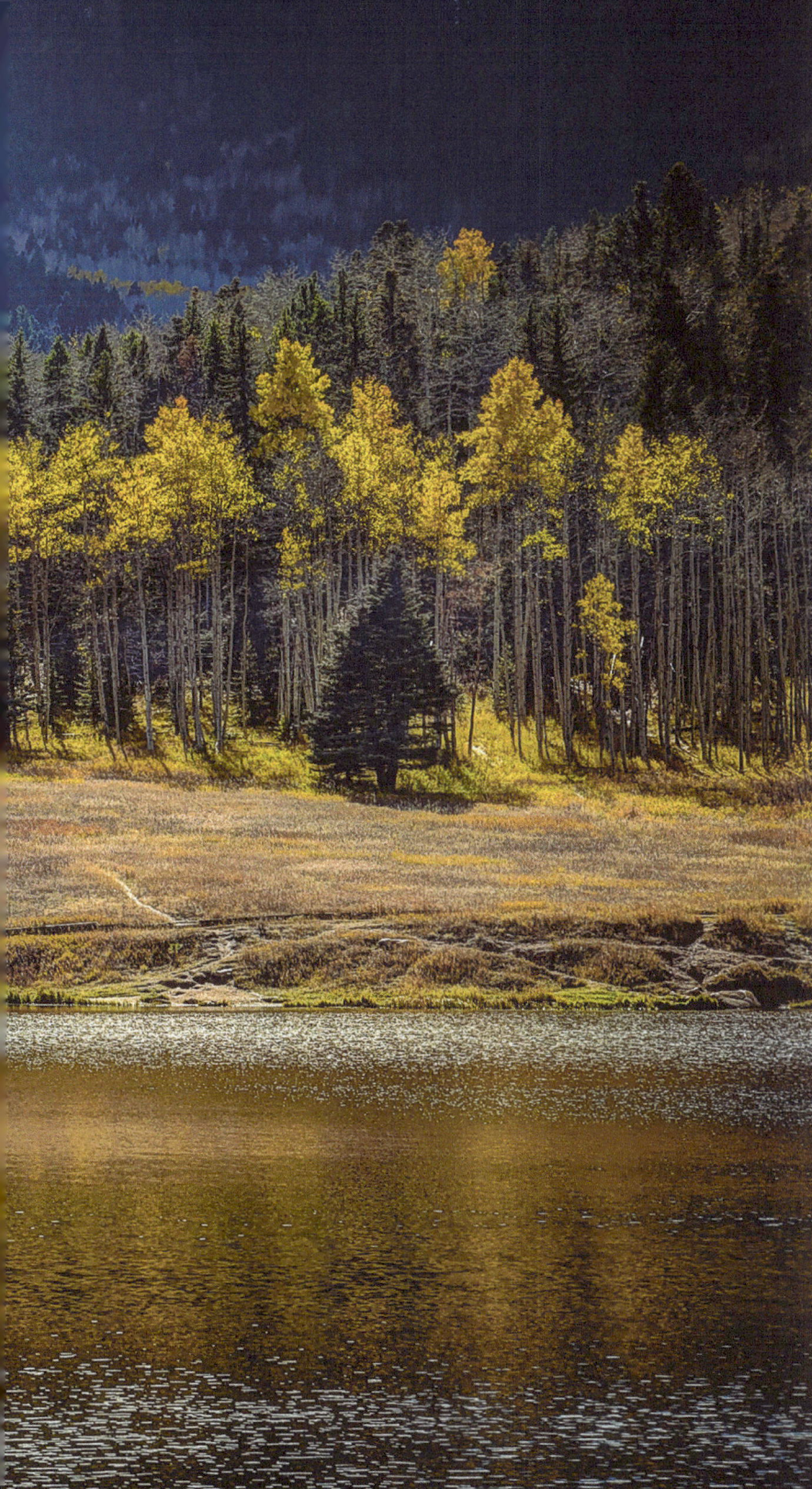

One of the most beautiful sights I have ever seen in the fall can be found in the mountains of Colorado.

Nestled among the evergreens, I marvel at the sight of a stand of aspen trees huddled together, their leaves a brilliant yellow or bright orange contrasting strikingly midst a sea of green. But have you ever wondered why you seldom see a lone aspen tree? They are almost always found in a group of other aspens with identical traits. Aspens are communal trees that live in clonal colonies—a group of genetically identical individuals that grow together and originate from the same parent seedling. New shoots start from root suckers that garner nourishment and pull life from the parent. These new trees clone distinguishing characteristics from the parent plant, therefore sharing traits like the same leaf shape, tree size, and bark character. These communities of trees share the same root system and are dependent upon one

LAKE ISABEL,
PUEBLO COUNTY,
COLORADO

another. Because they share the same root system, aspens are less likely to blow over in strong winds than non-communal trees. The intricate root system helps the trees stand firm when the winds blow.

Nature can teach us a lot through these communities of trees. The word "community" says it all. Community is actually a compound word: "com" means with, and "unity" means just that, unity. Psalm 133:1 (NIV) says, *"How good and pleasant it is when God's people live together in unity."* This verse doesn't mean we all have to agree with one another on everything, but we do need to be like-minded in Christ. Philippians 2:2–4 (NIV) admonishes us to *"then make my joy complete by being like-minded, having the same love, being one in spirit and of one mind. Do nothing out of selfish ambition or vain conceit. Rather, in humility value others above yourselves, not looking to your own interests but each of you to the interests of the others."*

Galatians 6:2 (ESV) says, *"Bear one another's burdens and so fulfill the Law of Christ."* Like the aspens, we need to depend on one another, to encourage one another, and to lean on one another to help us withstand the winds of change. If one of us is struggling, we need to help carry the burden. If one of us is discouraged, we need to love and encourage him. As a community of believers, we need to stand together. There is strength in numbers. We are stronger together than we are as individuals. If the aspens know this, so should we. Let's learn this lesson from nature and do like the aspens. ❧

11

Burn the Ships

"Remember not the former things, nor consider the things of old. Behold, I am doing a new thing; now it springs forth, do you not perceive it? I will make a way in the wilderness and rivers in the desert."

ISAIAH 43:18-19 (ESV)

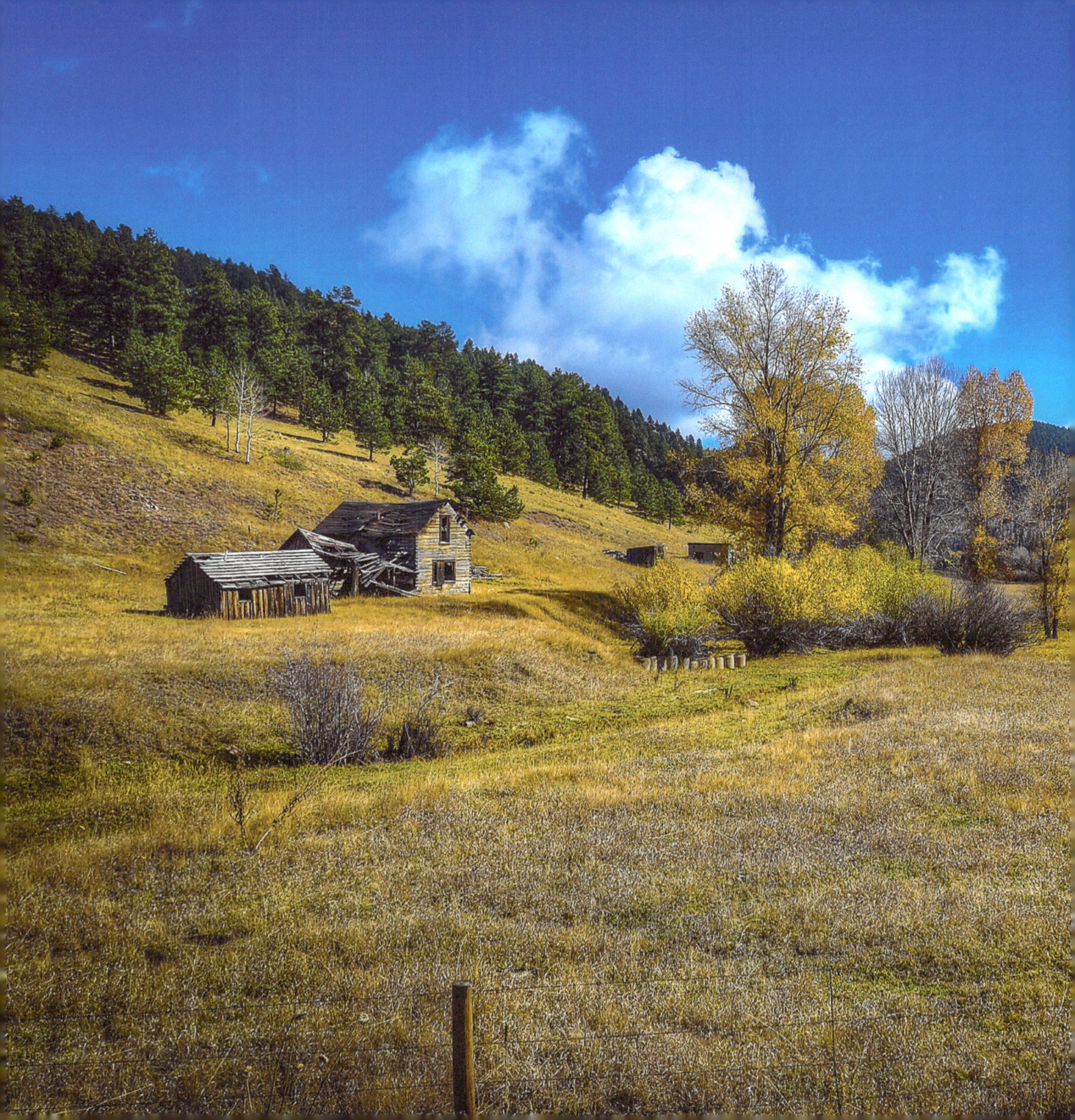

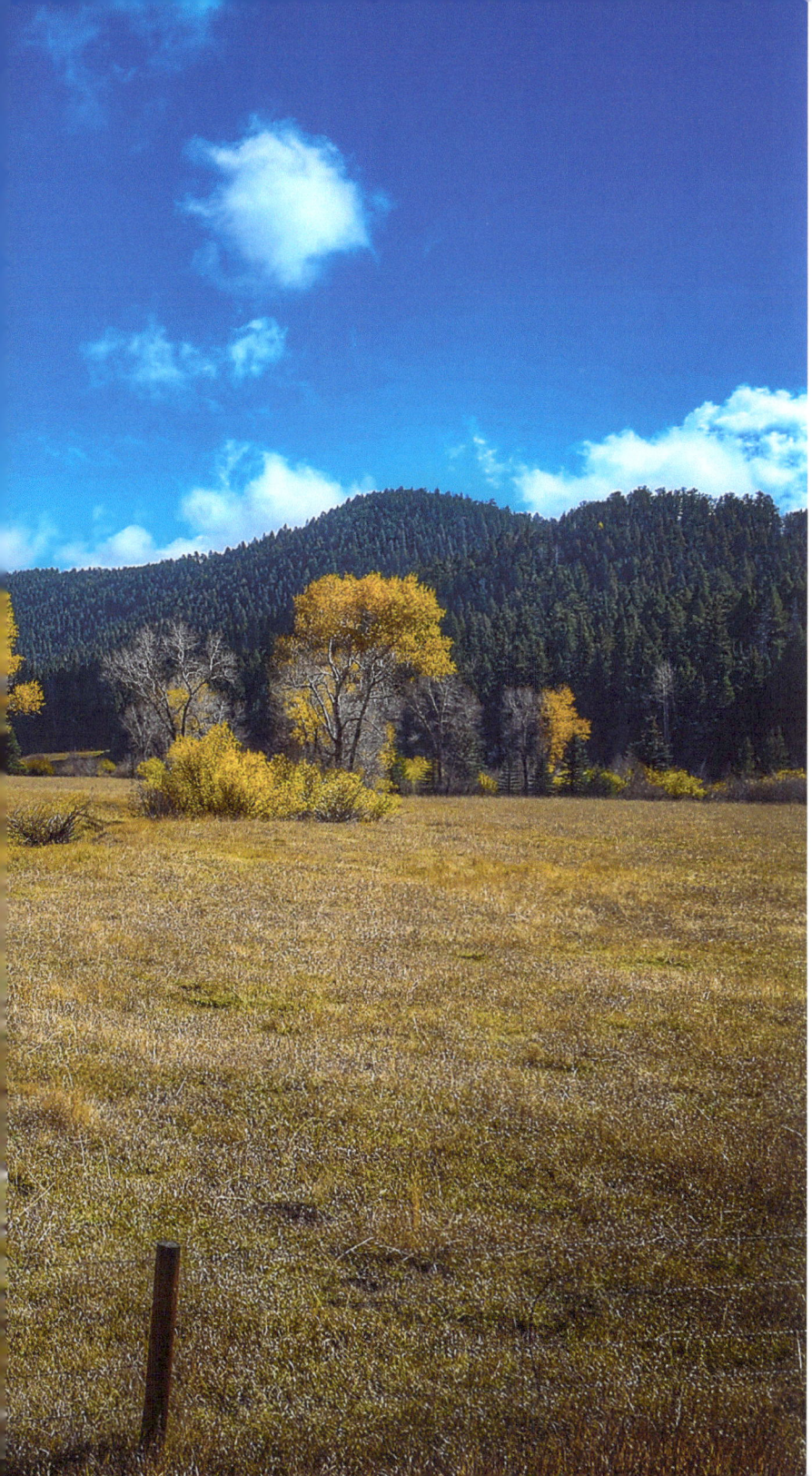

In the spring of 1519, Hernán Cortés, a Spanish conquistador, led a troop of approximately 500 soldiers in a fleet of eleven ships on a mission to Veracruz, Mexico.

His purpose was to overthrow Aztec emperor Montezuma II and take control of his vast wealth. Cortés was well aware that for the past 600 years, other conquerors, most with greater resources than he had, had attempted to colonize the Yucatán Peninsula without success. Knowing this, he took a different approach to battle. Instead of jumping immediately into battle the minute they docked their boats, he held his men on the beach and encouraged them through a series of valiant speeches that touched their souls and fed their thirst for victory. As they marched inland into battle, Cortés

ABANDONED CABIN, CUSTER COUNTY, COLORADO

ordered his troops to "burn the boats." This was a risky move. If the battle didn't go in their favor, the men were left without any place to go to save their lives. Cortés's command to burn the boats left his men with only two choices—succeed or die. Failure was not an option. There was to be no retreat. He knew it. They knew it. And it proved to be the wisest strategy necessary for success.

So what can we learn from this? Many of us hold on to something "just in case." We cling to the past as if letting go and pressing onward will send us down a path of destruction. We look back at the way things were, and we yearn for those days because they were familiar. It is easy to retreat if we know retreat is an option. Take the Israelites for example. In the first days, as Moses led them out of Egypt, the Israelites were ecstatic. Their days of slavery and persecution were finally over. The Lord had heard their cries and had delivered them. No longer were they living under the harsh rule of the Egyptians. However, as time went on and things got difficult, they began to yearn for the past. *In the desert the whole community grumbled against Moses and Aaron. The Israelites said to them, 'If only we had died by the Lord's hand in Egypt! There we sat around pots of meat and ate all the food we wanted, but you have brought us out into this desert to starve this entire assembly to death'* (Exodus 16:1–3, NIV). They did not know what the future held. They didn't know where they would find water or their next meal. They began to yearn for the past. In a mere two months and fifteen days of moving forward into the unknown with Moses and Aaron, the Israelites longed for their former life—a life of tyranny under Pharaoh's reign in Egypt. How quickly they forgot the *reality* of their former life. They focused on what they had, instead of moving forward toward what was being offered to them. They viewed the past through rose-colored glasses and ignored the reality of how it once was and how God's hand had worked to deliver them.

In the same way, God urges us to keep moving forward today. He wants us to keep our eyes on Him, *"forgetting what lies behind and reaching forward to what lies ahead"* as we *"press on toward the goal for the prize of the upward call of God in Christ Jesus"* (Philippians 3:13–14, NIV).

Ask yourself the following questions: "Do I have ships in my life that I need to burn?" "Are there things that I am afraid to let go of?" "Is there anything holding me back? Keeping me from pressing on toward the goal?" Ask God to reveal the answer to those questions, deal with His response, and move forward. *"For I know the plans I have for you,"* declares the Lord, *"plans to prosper you and not to harm you, plans to give you hope and a future"* (Jeremiah 29:11, NIV). Go ahead. Take God at His word and let go of the past. The future lies ahead of you and is waiting to be discovered. You never know; you just might like what you discover there. ❧

12

Through the Waters

"Do not fear, for I have redeemed you; I have summoned you by name; you are mine. When you pass through the waters, I will be with you; and when you pass through the rivers, they will not sweep over you. When you walk through the fire, you will not be burned; the flames will not set you ablaze."

ISAIAH 43:1–2 (NIV)

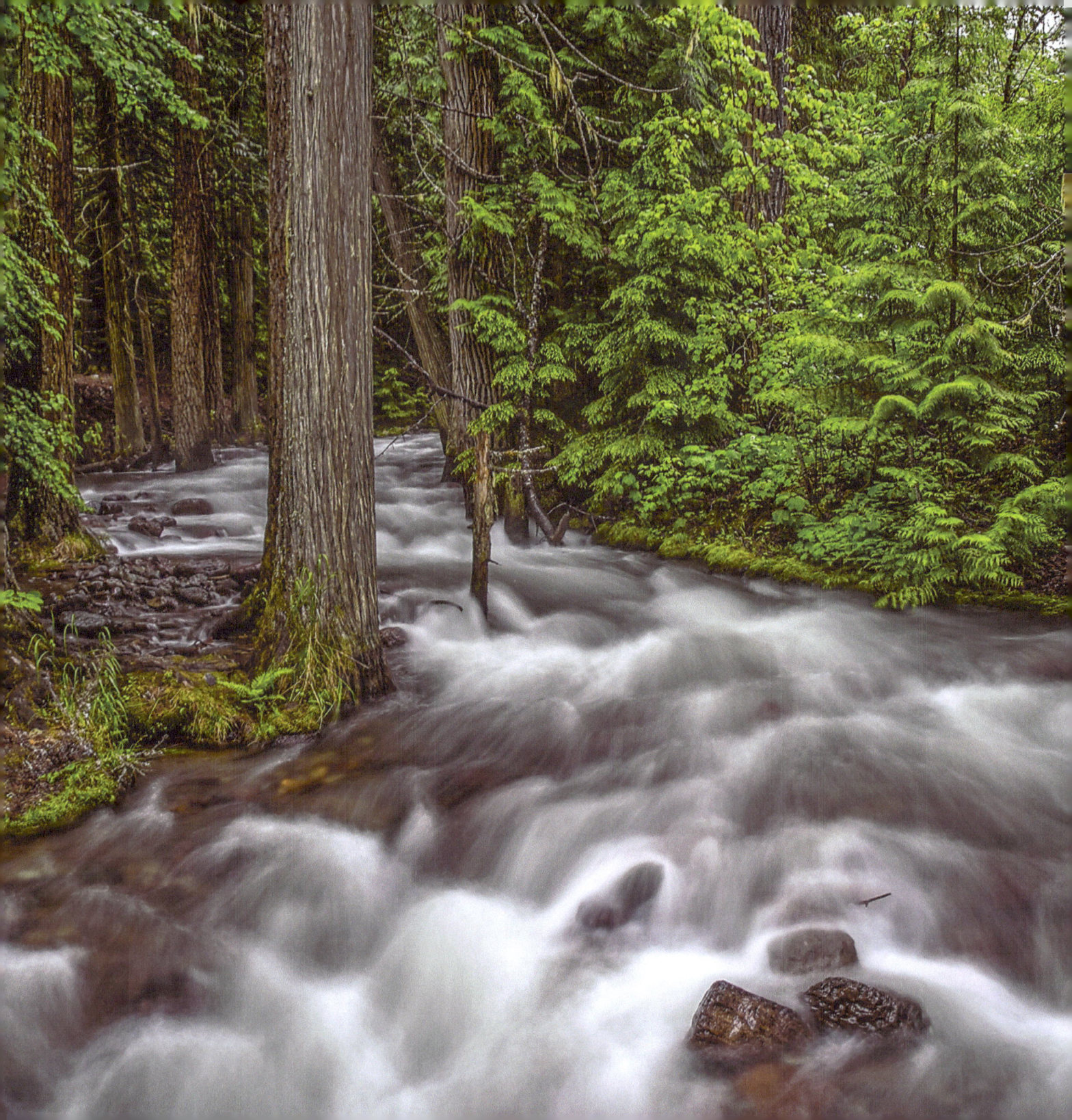

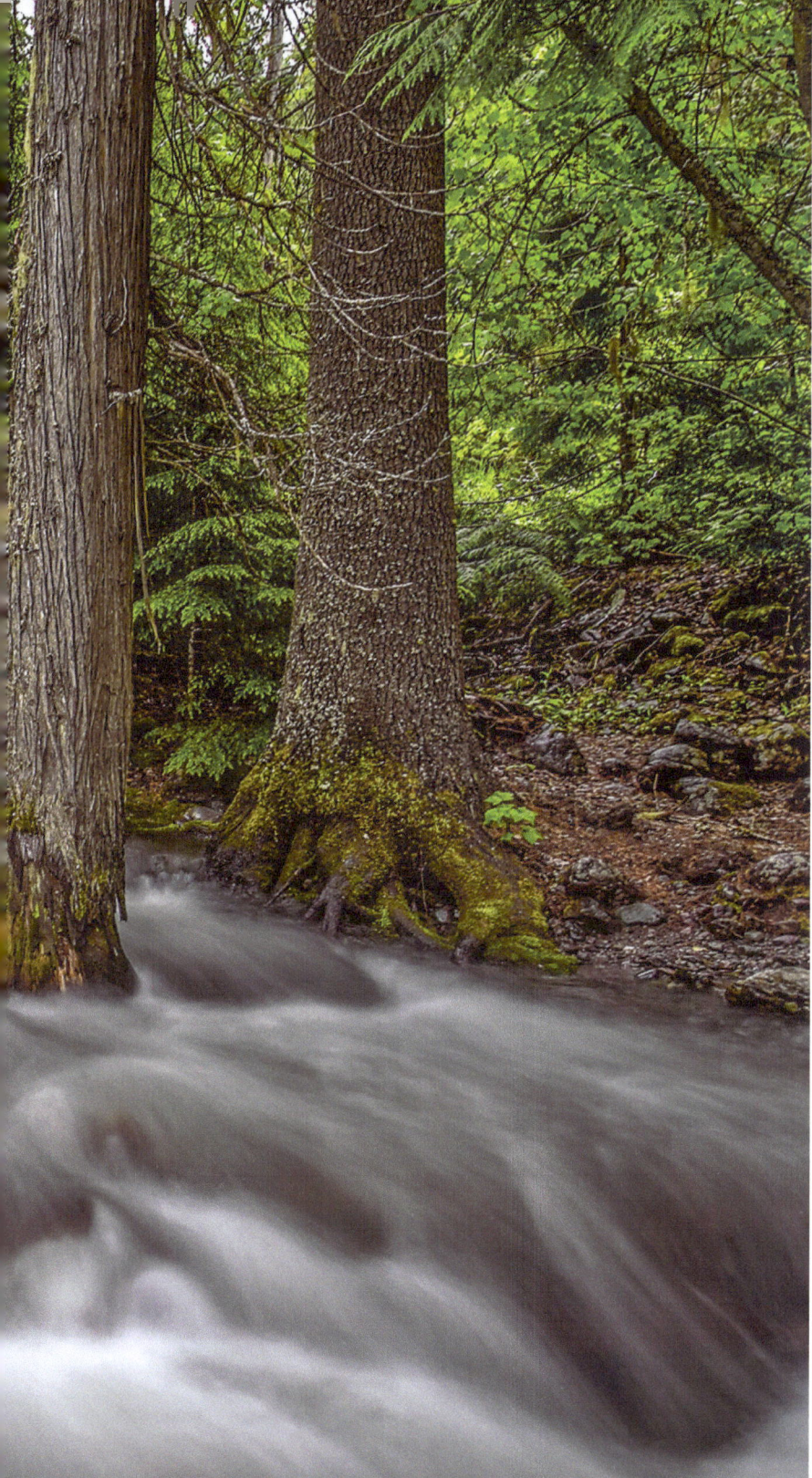

Isaiah 43 speaks to everyone who has ever made a mistake; to everyone who has ever gone in the opposite direction of God's will; to everyone who has ever breathed a breath.

"For all have sinned and fall short of the glory of God" (Romans 3:23, NIV). The previous portions of this passage in Isaiah tell how the people of Israel had fallen away from the path on which God was leading them. They would not walk in God's ways; they were disobedient. When corrected by Him, they were stubborn and still refused to listen and obey. Human logic would say, "I'm done with them. I tried, but they just won't listen. I wash my hands of them." However, God doesn't work that way. Instead He tells them, *"Do not fear, for I have redeemed you . . ."* God is a loving

SNYDER CREEK, GLACIER
NATIONAL PARK, MONTANA

and gracious God and wants nothing more than for His children to live full and prosperous lives of obedience in Him. Despite their ungratefulness and disobedience, God continued to care for His people and take care of them. That truth still stands with us today. God cares for us and promises to take care of us.

Notice that in this passage, God does not promise us a life of luxury. There is no mention of a bed of roses. He doesn't say there won't be rough times. Instead He instructs us, *"Do not fear . . ."* He offers to guide and direct us, to take care of us when the path gets rocky. He promises to be with us when we walk through rough waters. He promises to take care of us as we pass through the moments of difficulty. He knows that there will be times of trouble in our lives, some of which are inadvertently brought on by ourselves, but He promises to be with us through it all. It is during those times of trouble that we must continue to praise Him and seek His will. It is during those troubling times that we need to lean on Him the most.

The most encouraging part of this passage comes at the end of verse one. *". . . I have summoned you by name; you are mine."* There is something significant about having someone call you by name. It says, "You are unique. You are important. You are special." We are God's creation. We belong to Him. He knows each one of us by name, and He cares for each of us as though we are the only one that matters. We can take comfort in knowing that God knows us by name. When we face hardship and take our first steps into the rushing water, we need to listen for the voice of God to call out our names. When we praise Him for his care and guidance, we can reach up and grab the protective and loving hand of the God who knows us like no other. ☙

13

Stand Firm

"Therefore, my beloved brethren, be steadfast, immovable, always abounding in the work of the Lord, knowing that your toil is not in vain in the Lord."

1 CORINTHIANS 15:58 (BLB)

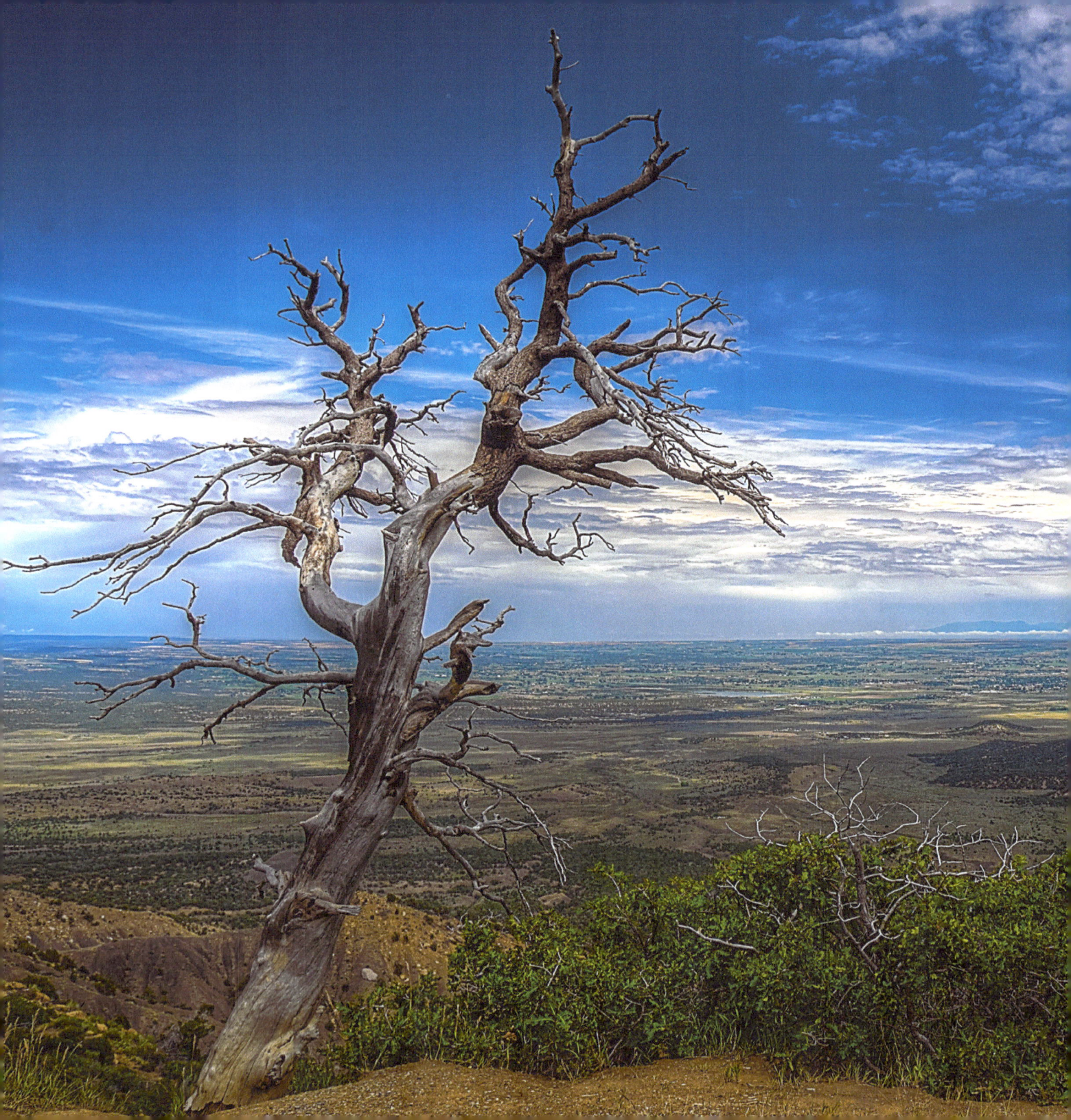

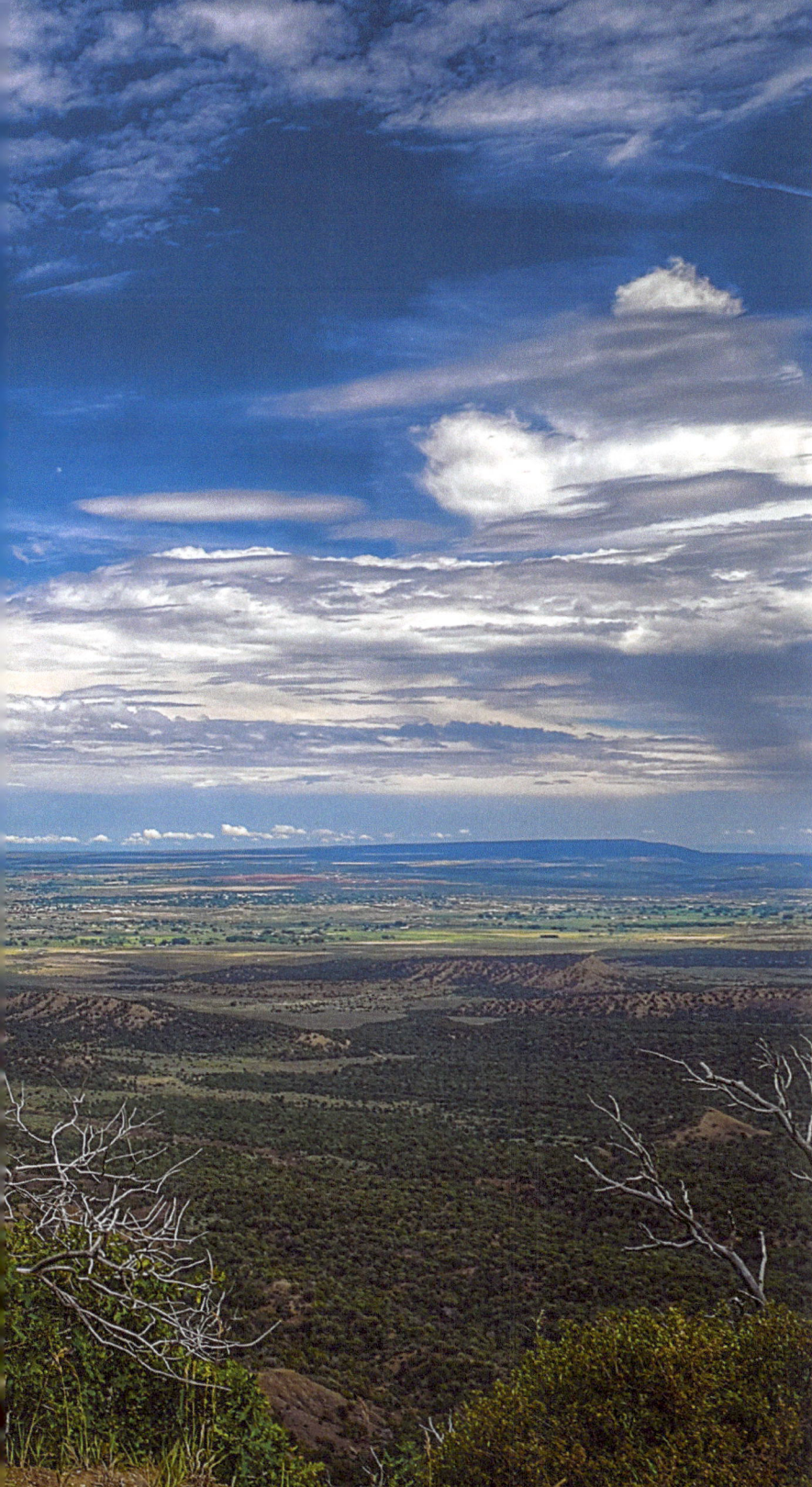

The word "steadfast" means to be firmly fixed in place.

It means remaining loyal, faithful, committed, and devoted. We all know people who are die-hard fans of their favorite sports team. They remain true to their team regardless of the scoreboard. There is something powerful about rooting for their team whether the team is winning or losing. They hold on to the hope that this will be the year, or the next play will turn the tides in their team's favor. Their faith never wavers, regardless of the current situation their team is facing.

The Bible tells countless stories of believers standing firm when circumstances were not in their favor. Shadrach, Meshach, and Abed-Nego were examples of believers who were steadfast in their faith even when their very lives were at stake. Daniel, too, held fast to his faith even when he knew the law demanded otherwise. In more recent days, believers at Umpqua Community College in Roseburg, Oregon, held firm to their faith in the face of imminent death. As the gunman reloaded his weapon after shooting a college professor at point-blank range, the shooter asked the students in the class

WEATHERED CEDAR TREE, BLACK CANYON OF THE GUNNISON NATIONAL PARK, COLORADO

to stand, then asked if they were Christians. Upon hearing their affirmative answers, the gunman replied, "Good, because you're a Christian, you're going to see God in just about one second," and then he shot them. Nine students lost their lives in that attack. They held steadfast—immovable in the face of danger—and did not waver in their faith. In that moment, did they lose their lives? No! They gained eternal life with their Savior Jesus Christ!

Thankfully most of us will never face situations like the one that happened in Oregon. Yet time and again we have encountered situations where we should have remained steadfast. When fear reared its ugly head, we wavered. We knew we should have stood firm, but we second-guessed ourselves and took a different, seemingly safer road instead. We have faced times where doubt entered our minds and caused us to pause or change paths. The thief who seeks to steal and kill and destroy put doubt there. When that happened, we let those seeds of doubt blur our vision, and we lost sight of the path on which we should have trod.

In our daily lives we long for affirmation and approval from those around us even though the Bible instructs us to put our faith in God, not in man. When that affirmation doesn't come, seeds of doubt are planted. It is during those times of doubt that we need to look up. Look up to the God, who set the universe into motion, and trust that our toil is not in vain. If God is for us, who can be against us? (Romans 8:31, NIV). ❧

14

Down the Right Path

"Trust in the Lord with all your heart and lean not on your own understanding; in all your ways acknowledge Him, and He will direct your path."

PROVERBS 3:5 (ESV)

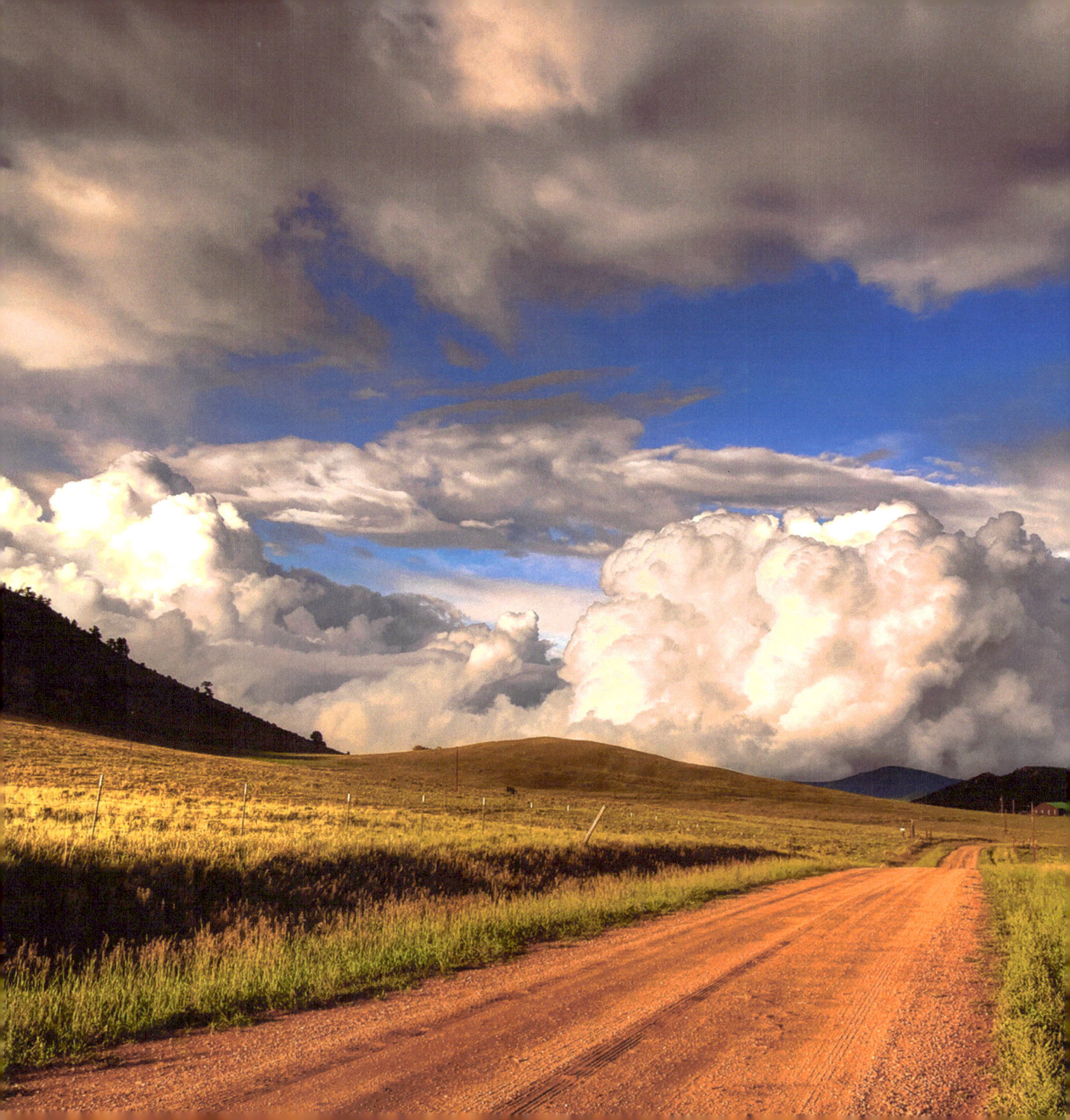

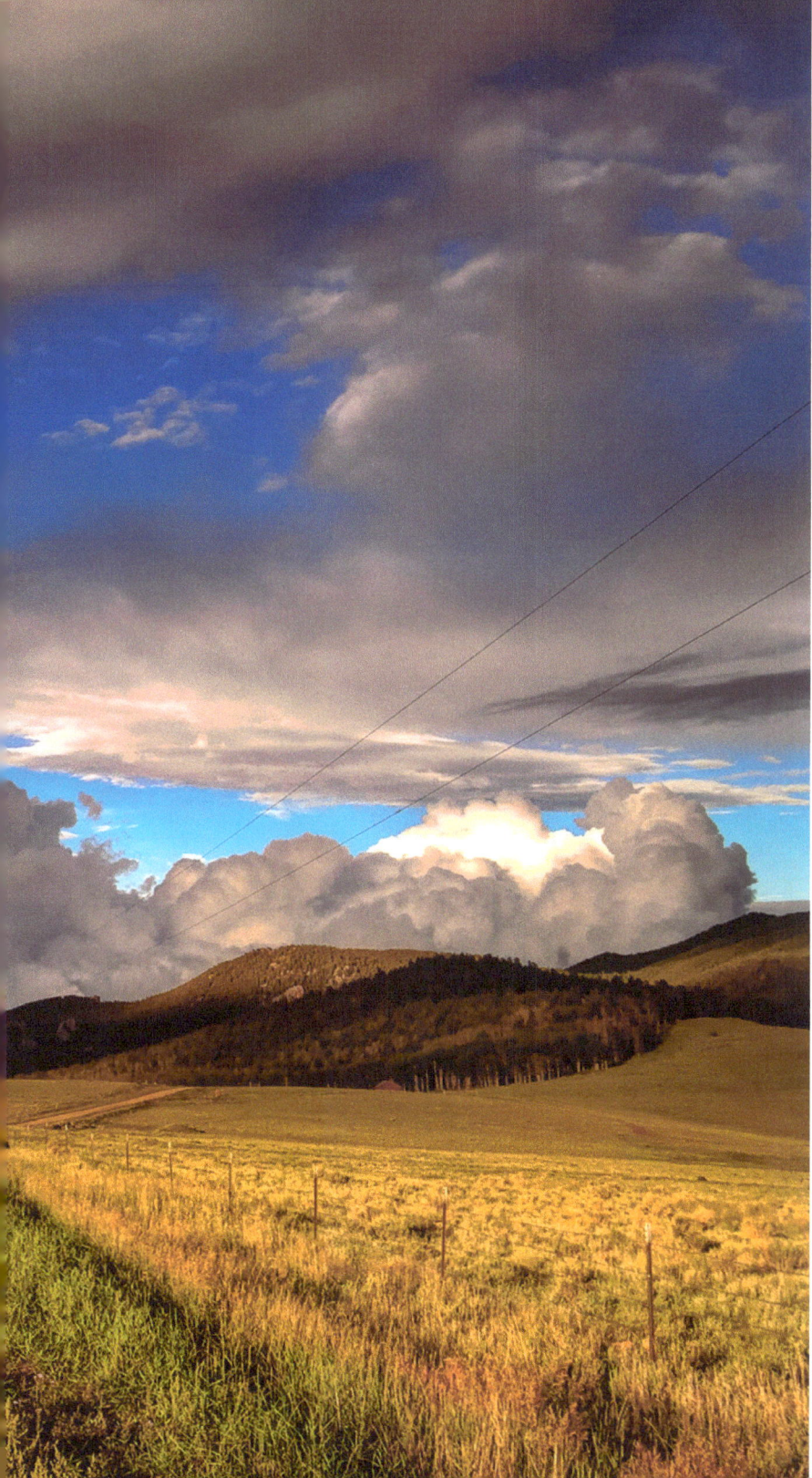

Someone once said that the average human being makes approximately 35,000 remotely conscious decisions each and every day.

We make decisions from the moment we get up in the morning to the moment we fall asleep at night. Those decisions cover a wide variety of areas: What should I wear? What should I eat? What exit do I need to take? No matter the type or topic of the decision, the fact still remains that our brain is called upon to make a multitude of decisions throughout the day. Fortunately most of the decision-making process happens so seamlessly that we often don't even realize we've made a decision until after the fact.

There are different types of decision-makers. Some decision-makers are impulsive. They take the first solution that comes their way without fully considering the potential consequences that could arise. Others are more methodical.

MOUNTAIN ROAD, CUSTER COUNTY, COLORADO

These are the people who think about all of the potential consequences—sometimes dreaming up consequences that probably don't even exist in the first place—and weigh all the consequences before making a final decision. Then there are the non-decision-makers. These are the people who are so indecisive or fearful of making a decision that they end up making no decision, which, in itself, is ultimately a decision whether they want to admit it or not. In other instances, depending on the situation, some decision-makers do a combination of all three. Decisions are a part of life, and like it or not, we will find ourselves faced with the task of making them.

Decision-making undoubtedly puts a great load of stress on our shoulders. But it doesn't have to be stressful. Proverbs 3:5 (KJV) tells us to *"trust in the Lord . . . and He will direct our paths."* We can lean on God, knowing that He hears us. Too often we forget that God cares about us and has promised to help us through the tough moments of life. We must not forget the key piece of Proverbs 3:5, however. The middle part of the verse says, *". . . lean not on our own under-standing . . ."* Even when things are confusing, and we can't understand our situation, we can trust that, when asked, God will give us direction. But we must ask. Prayer is crucial in times like these. We cannot forget the power of prayer when faced with decisions. Philippians 4:6 (NASB) says, *"Be anxious for nothing, but in everything by prayer and supplication, with thanksgiving, let your requests be made known to God."* If we take God at His word, we can bring our petitions to God knowing that He hears our cries. The best part comes next. Philippians 4:7 continues with, *"Then the peace of God that surpasses all understanding will guard your hearts and minds in Christ Jesus."* Bringing our petitions to God, *with thanksgiving*, will yield a peace we cannot get anywhere else.

The next time we are faced with the task of making tough decisions, we must take our requests to Him in prayer and thanksgiving, and ask that He will direct our paths. God has a different vantage point than we do. He sees a bigger picture and will guide us down the right path. That is a comforting thought we can carry with us as we journey down this path called life. ☙

15

Great Is Thy Faithfulness

"Because of the Lord's great love we are not consumed, for his compassions never fail. They are new every morning; great is your faithfulness. I say to myself, 'The Lord is my portion; therefore I will wait for him.'"

Lamentations 3:22–23 (NIV)

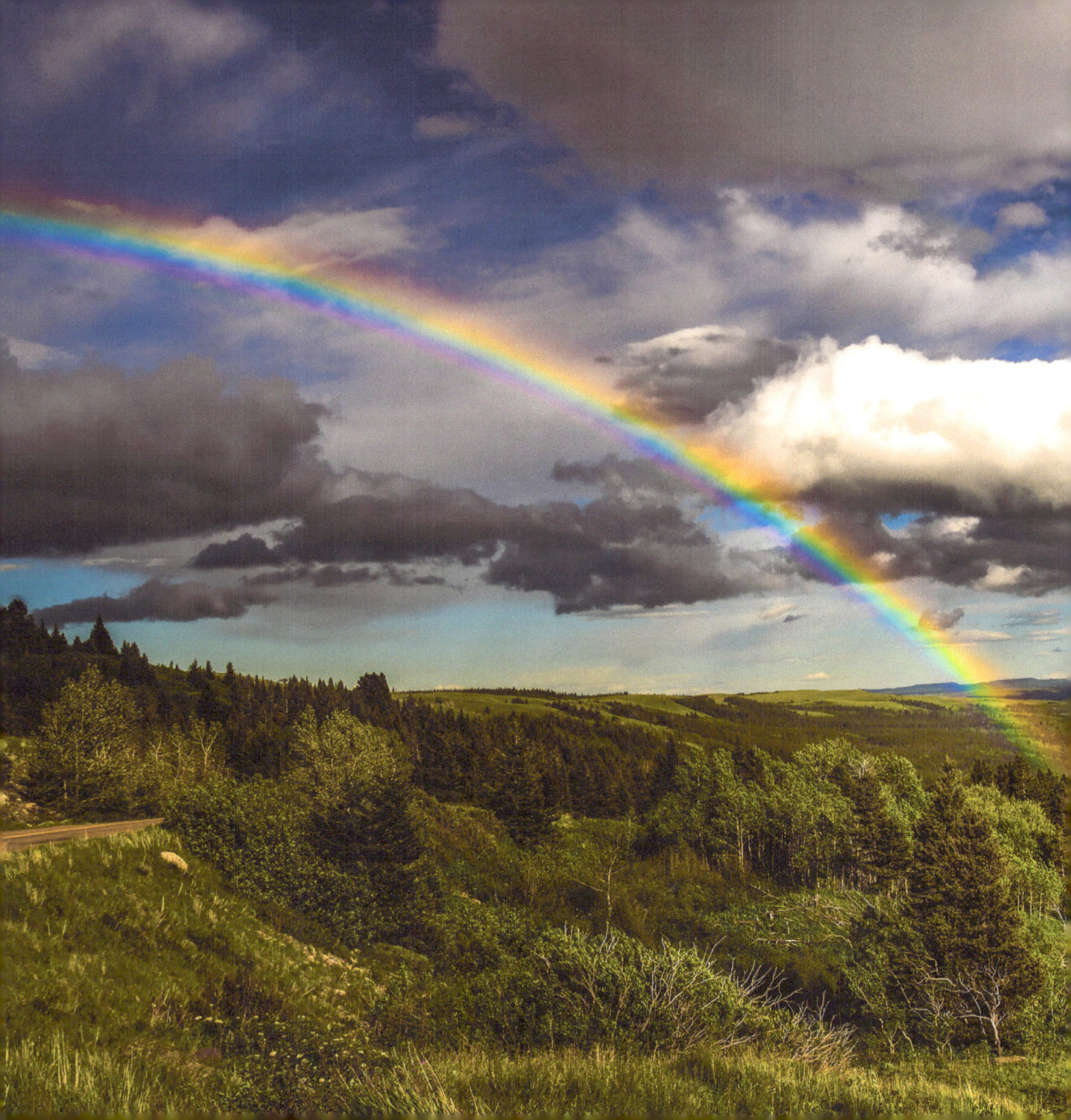

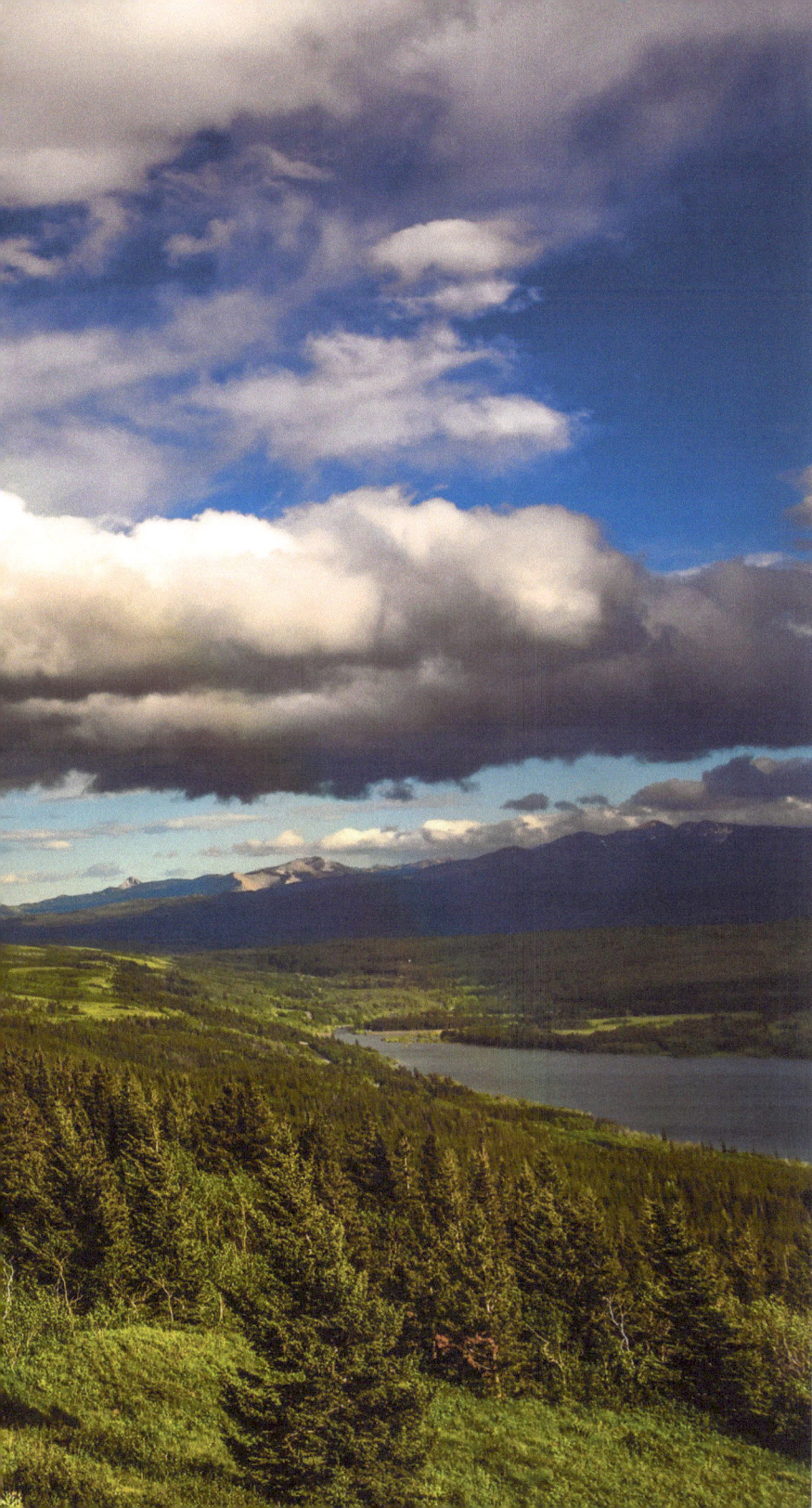

When tragedy strikes, people often ask the question "why?"

It is understandable to question "why?" or ask "when will this all end?" and "what is the world coming to?" Hearts break when media reports are filled with stories of death, destruction, heartache, and misery. Sometimes fear even fills our hearts when we hear reports that hit a little too close to home. However, God instructs us, "do not fear."

Satan is working overtime to cause calamity in our world and would like nothing more than to convince people that he is in control. But we have a hope we can cling to. Proverbs 19:21 (ESV) tells us *"Many are the plans in the mind of a man, but it is the purpose of the Lord that will stand."* Hallelujah! Praise the Lord, for His promises are true! Look at the promise in this verse: *". . . it is the purpose of the Lord that will stand."* Do you see it? It doesn't matter what man does to cause unrest and insecurity, because God's purpose will prevail.

Joshua 1:9 (ESV) holds another promise. *"Have I not commanded you? Be strong and courageous. Do not be frightened, and do not be dismayed, for*

GOD'S PROMISE REMINDER,
GLACIER NATIONAL PARK,
MONTANA

the Lord your God is with you wherever you go." These are the times when it is most imperative that we cling to the hope of God's promises.

In Isaiah 45:6–7 (NIV) we are reminded, *"I am the Lord, and there is no other; apart from me there is no God. I will strengthen you, though you do not acknowledge me, so that from the rising of the sun, to the place of its setting people may know there is none beside me. I am the Lord and there is no other."* Bad things may happen, but God will not let any of this go unpunished.

We who hold steadfast to our faith and hold on to the hope of His promises will not be consumed.

"Behold, He is coming with the clouds, and every eye will see Him, even those who pierced Him, and all tribes of the earth will wail on account of Him. Even so. Amen. 'I am the Alpha and the Omega,' says the Lord God, 'who is and who was and who is to come, the Almighty'" (Revelations 1:7–8 NIV). In these troubling days, there is no greater promise than that. Rest in His promises and trust in His faithfulness. ⚘

16

Just Passing Through

"Do not let your hearts be troubled. Trust in God; trust also in me. In my Father's house are many rooms; if it were not so, I would have told you. I am going there to prepare a place for you. And if I go and prepare a place for you, I will come back and take you to be with me that you also may be where I am."

JOHN 14:1-3 (ESV)

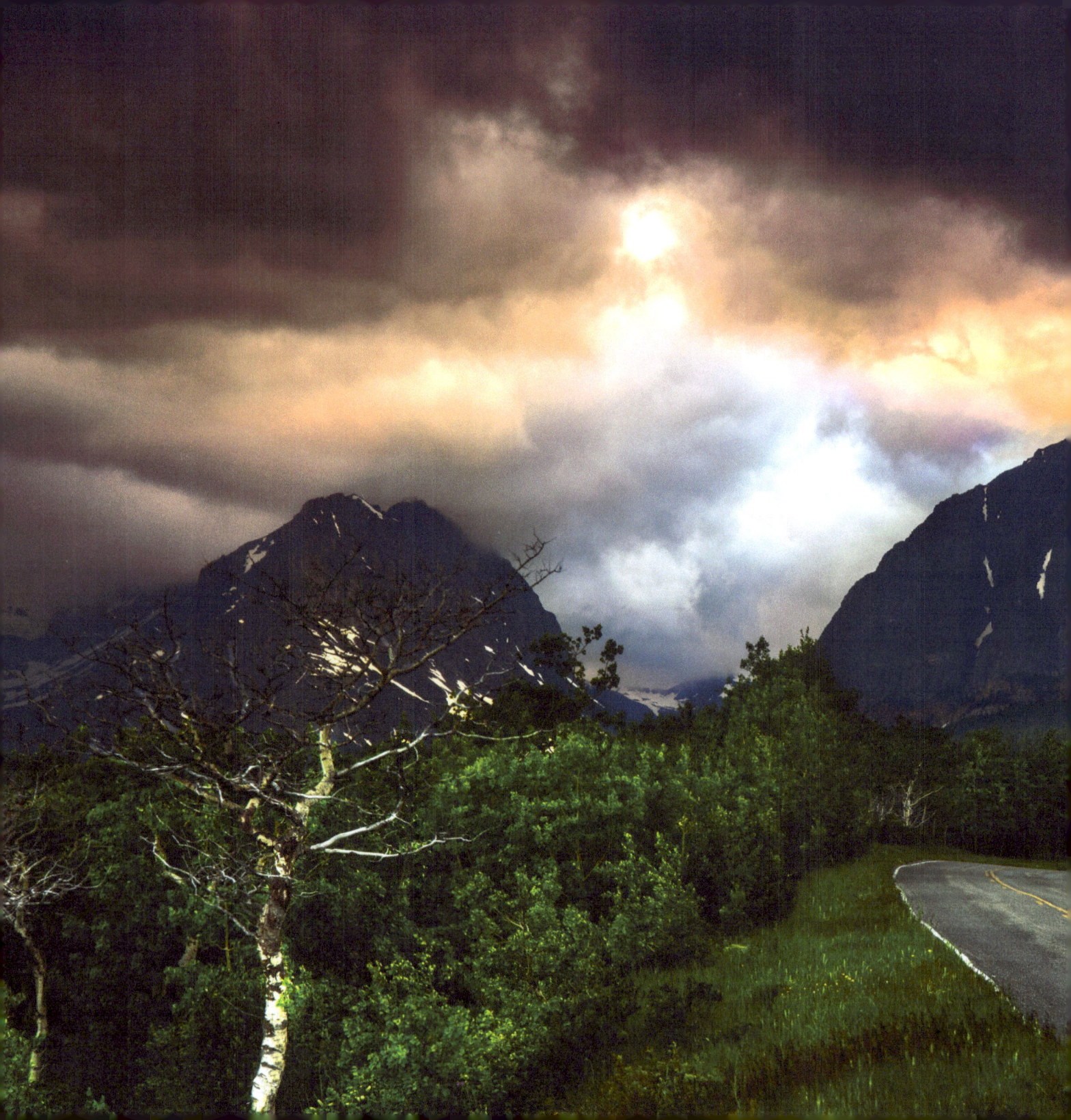

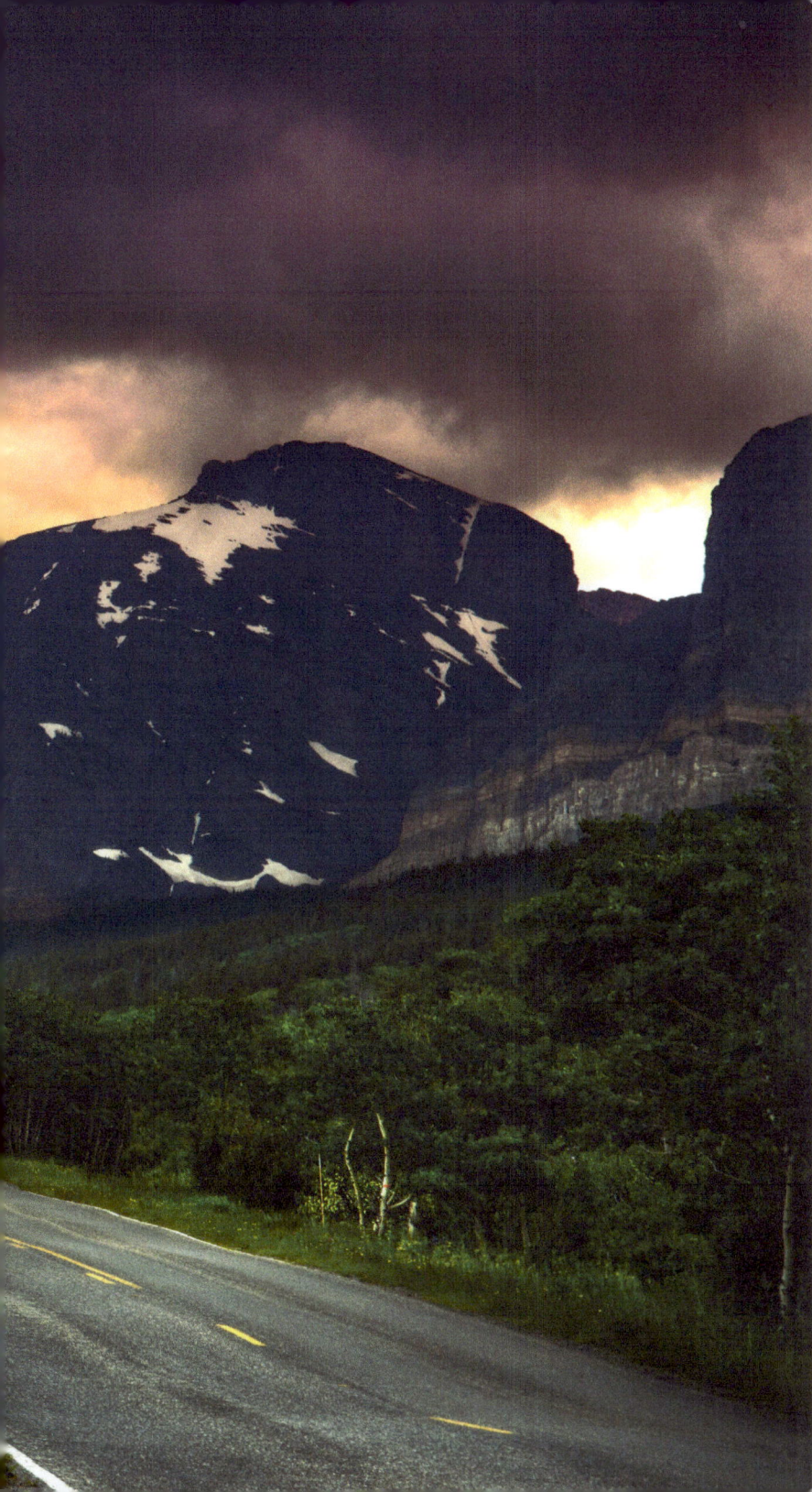

Jesus was a carpenter.

His words in John 14 tell us He is preparing a place for us. A carpenter—preparing a place for us! This is exciting news! Jesus told his disciples not to let their hearts be troubled because He was leaving them for a while. His purpose? To prepare a place for them. If you like great architecture, these words ought to be pretty exciting. Think about it. Jesus, a carpenter taught by the very one who created our incredible universe, is preparing a place for us right now, this very minute. Can you picture it? I have no doubt it will be amazing. Just read Revelation 21. The entire chapter is devoted to describing, in great detail, the city in which we will reside, and the picture those words paint is pretty amazing. How much more amazing will it be when we see it in person? If we trust in God and trust also in Jesus, we will one day walk along those streets of gold to the place that was prepared with us in mind.

The second part of this verse is just as exciting, however. The verse continues by saying, *"If I go and prepare a place for you, I will come back and take you to be with me . . ."* He's coming back! I love having Jesus in my heart and knowing that I can talk to Him and that He listens intently, but how much greater will it be to see Him face to face and have REAL

INTO THE STORM, GLACIER
NATIONAL PARK, MONTANA

heart-to-heart conversations with Him? My heart cannot contain the anticipation for that day.

So, what does that mean for us today? We are merely passing through this world in which we live. This is not our home. But we still have a responsibility to live fruitful lives—"fruitful" meaning productive. We are called to bring as many people as possible with us along the journey so that they, too, can go to the place Jesus is preparing. We can lead them by example; we can minister to them in their time of need; we can win them to Jesus by our steadfastness; we can pray; but most importantly, we can love them, as difficult as that may be at times. Our purpose here on Earth is to *"go and make disciples of all nations, baptizing them in the name of the Father and of the Son and of the Holy Spirit"* (Matthew 28:19, NIV). That is our calling. We must make use of every moment while we are passing through so that we can take as many with us as possible. ෆ

17

More Than Just a Hammer

"There are different kinds of gifts, but the same Spirit distributes them. There are different kinds of service, but the same Lord. There are different kinds of working, but in all of them and in everyone it is the same God at work."

1 CORINTHIANS 12:4-6 (NIV)

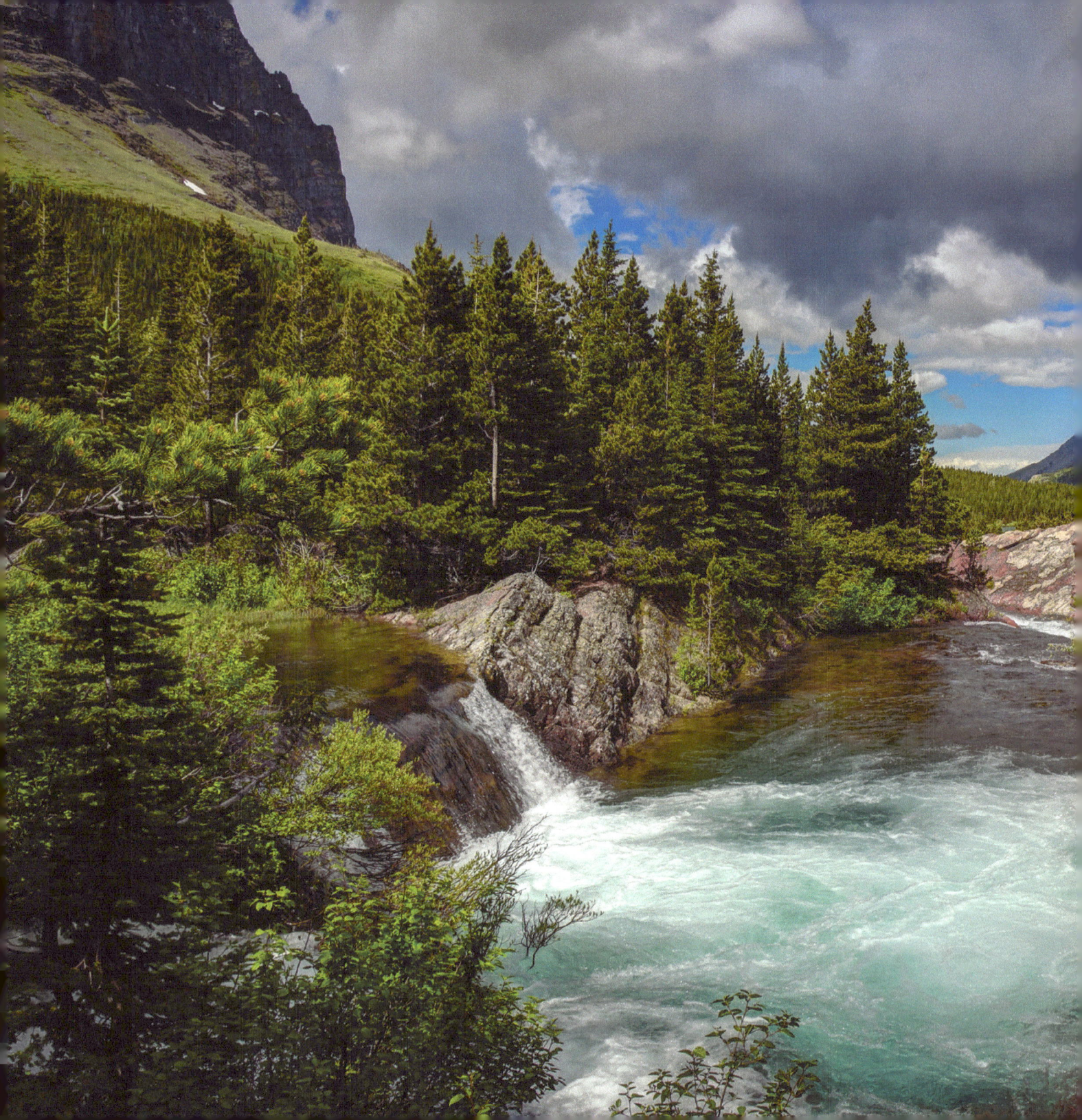

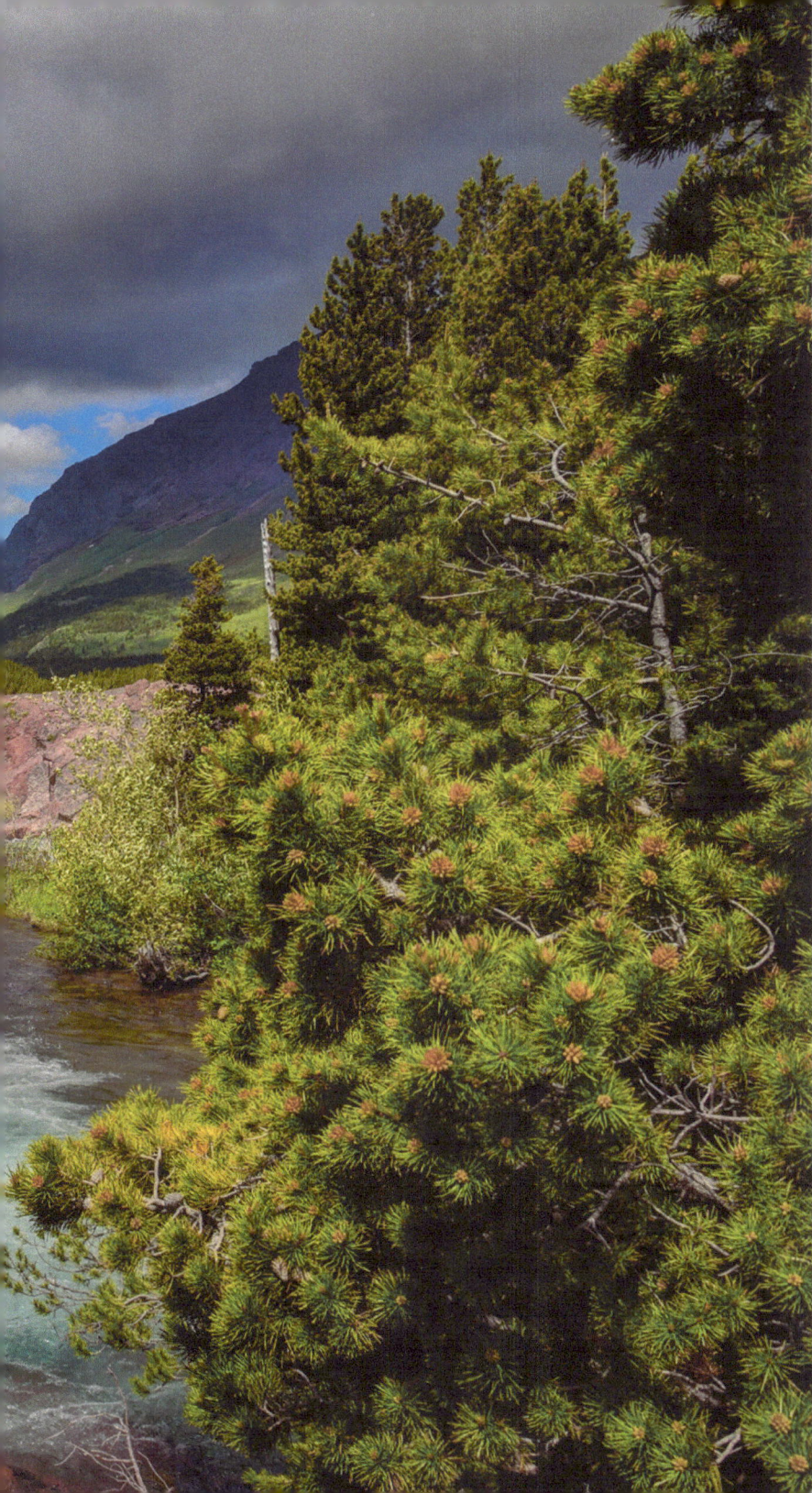

One of the most frequent questions I'm asked as a photographer is, "You take such beautiful pictures. What kind of camera do you use?"

When asked this, I'm tempted to give a smart-aleck response, but that wouldn't be nice, so I just give a straight answer and tell them what type of camera I use. What I really want to say, however, is, "It doesn't really matter." That response sounds a bit harsh, but it doesn't matter what camera a photographer uses. It is how a photograph is set up before the camera is used that matters. Think of it this way . . . When you see a beautifully crafted house, do you say to the carpenter, "Wow! That is a beautiful house. What kind of hammer did you use?" No, that would be absurd. You see, it isn't the tool that makes a house beautiful, it is the eye of the one who built it that makes all the difference.

We can use this anecdote as a

RED ROCK FALLS,
GLACIER NATIONAL
PARK, MONTANA

| 67

lesson regarding spiritual gifts. We are told in 1 Corinthians 12 that all are given special gifts to be used for the common good. Some are given wisdom, others are given miraculous powers, and others are given discerning minds, just to name a few. God determines to whom He will distribute these gifts. From there it is up to us to accept our gifts and use them according to His purpose.

Our gifts are different and each has its own defined purpose. Each gift is to be used to its full potential to further the kingdom of God. In the eyes of man, we tend to put an importance-value on our gifts. However, each gift is important; not one is more important than the other. We must resist the temptation to look at the gift we were given, compare it to the gift that someone else has, and then surmise that our gift isn't as good, or as important, or as effective. That line of thinking is of the devil and needs to be thwarted at all costs. Instead, we need to focus on doing the best we can at the job we were intended to do by using the gifts God has specifically given to us.

Now, let's look at the tools of the trade. It usually takes more than just the tool to get the job done. A good photographer not only uses a camera, he also uses a tripod, filters, a variety of different lenses, and photo editing software to perfect a photo. But it takes more than those tools to get a photo just right. The photographer also has to have the right mind-set and the right creative eye to visualize and set up a scene before ever taking the shot. Along the same line, a carpenter needs more than just tools to build a house. He can't build a beautiful house with just saws, nails, hammers, and other equipment. He has to have the vision, the blueprint, the know-how to get it done.

In the same way, God has prepared us to use the gift He has chosen for us. Were it not so, He wouldn't have entrusted us with the gift to begin with. It is our responsibility to fine-tune our gift—first by asking God for guidance and direction, and then by using it. We must remember, however, that no skill is ever perfected the first time it is tried. We will make mistakes. And when we do, we mustn't throw down our tool and give up on it altogether. On the contrary, it is when we make mistakes that we learn the most.

God expects us to use the tools He has provided so that we can further His kingdom. When we begin to see ourselves as servants of the Lord, set our eyes on the intended purpose, and begin to see the bigger picture, we become the instrument God desires for us to be. We must take a close look at ourselves and ask: Am I using the tools, the gifts God has given me? Am I using them to my full potential? Am I more than just a hammer? ✣

18

Sticks and Stones

"The heart of the wise instructs
his mouth . . ."

PROVERBS 16:23 (NASB)

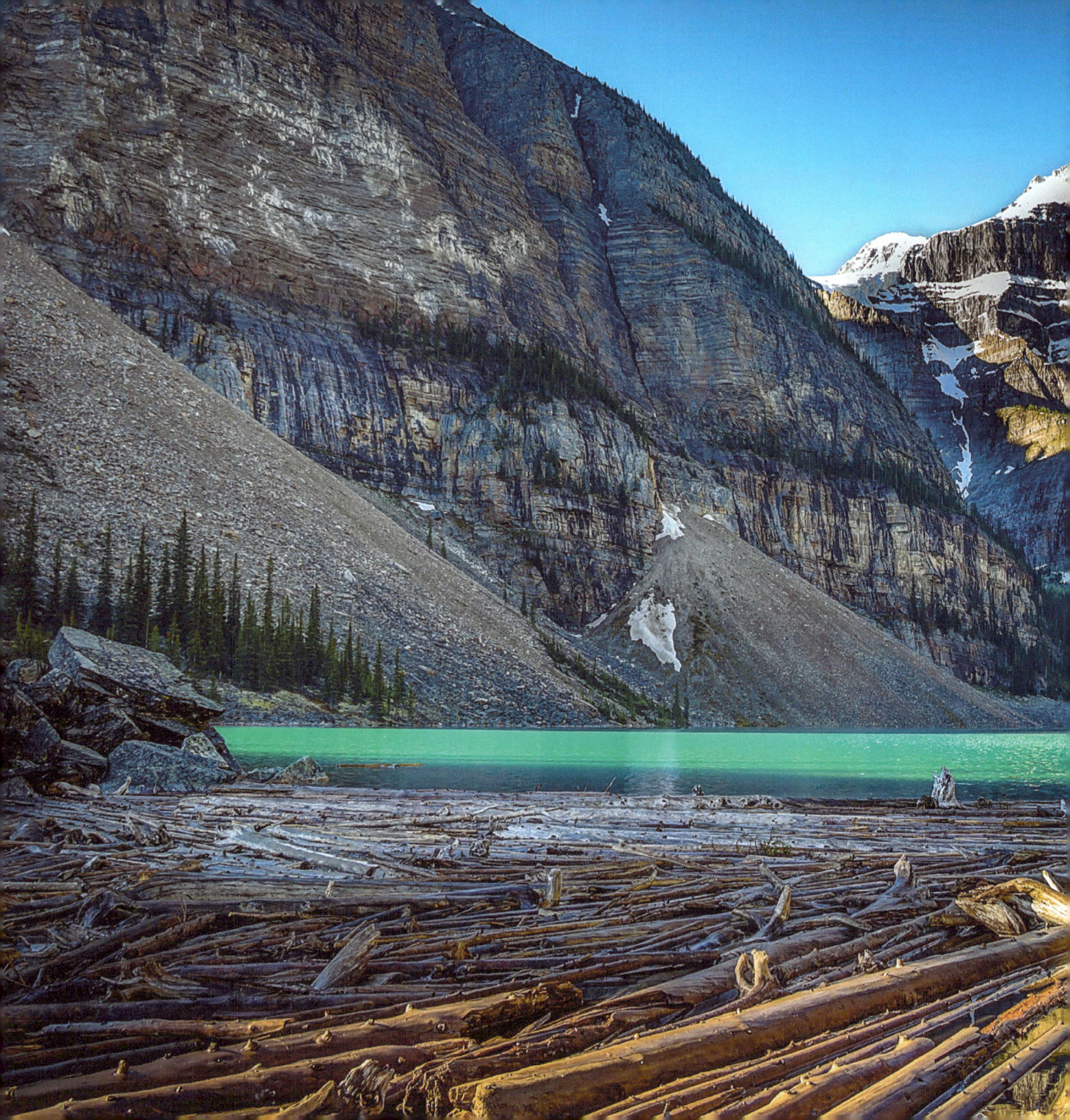

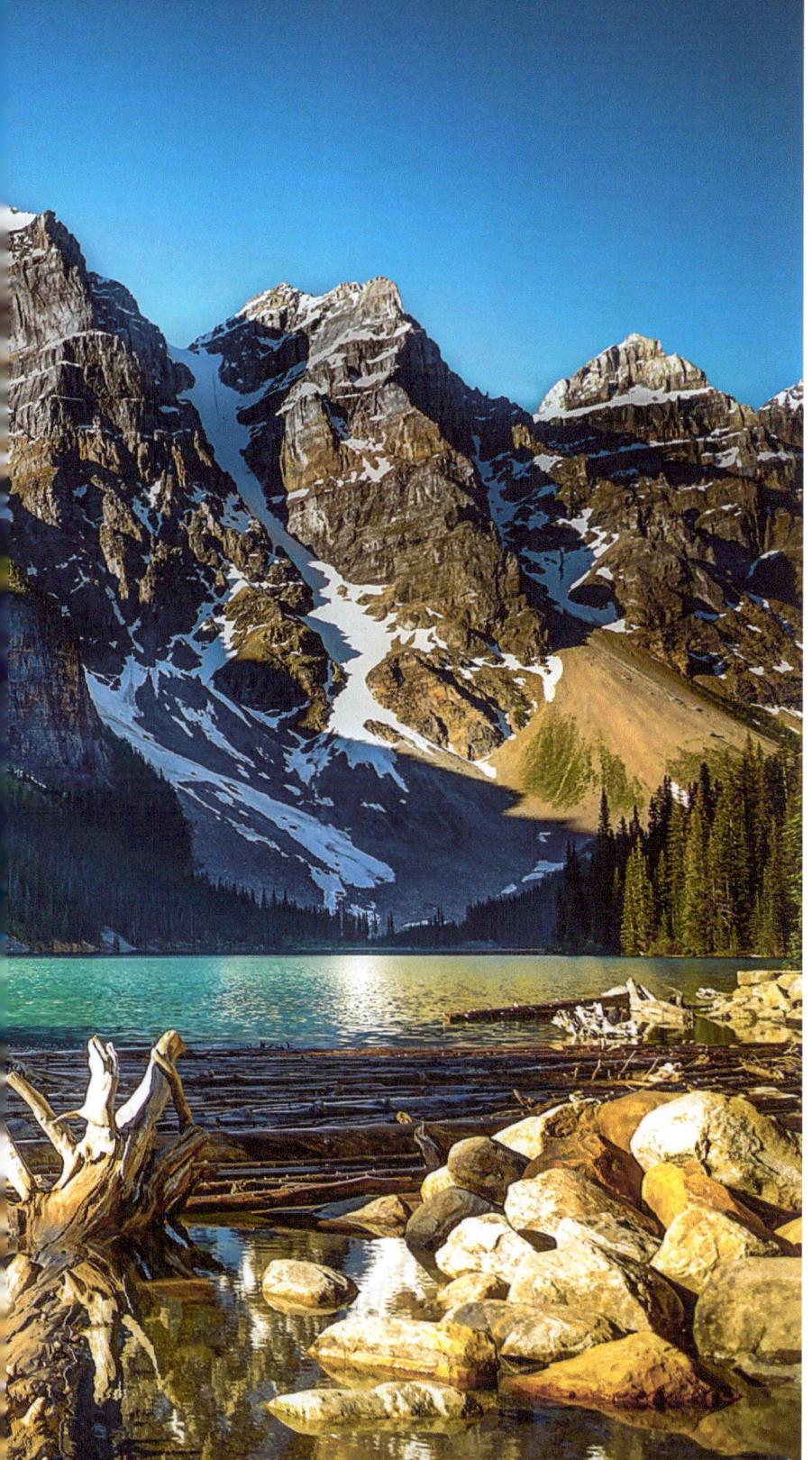

The first reported publication of the famous children's chant "sticks and stones can break my bones, but words can never hurt me" appeared in March 1862 in The Christian Recorder, published by the African Methodist Episcopal Church.

The supposed purpose of the phrase was to encourage children to ignore the taunting or childish name-calling of others. In principle, the adage sounds like pretty good advice, but in reality, it couldn't be any further from the truth. Words do hurt, and they hurt badly. Many relationships have been destroyed because of harsh words that were

MORAINE LAKE, BANFF NATIONAL PARK, ALBERTA, CANADA

spoken and never forgotten.

The words we say can do one of two things—they can do good, or they can do harm. In simpler terms, words can build up or tear down; they can encourage or defeat; they can show love or evil. Notice each has its opposite; there is no in-between. It is one or the other. Period. Once spoken, words can never be taken back. Words that hurt often hurt forever.

But where do those words come from? The mind? No, they come from the heart. Proverbs 16:23 says, *"The heart of the wise instructs his mouth."* But that isn't the only verse about the tongue. The Bible is full of verses that warn us to guard what comes out of our mouths:

"There is one whose rash words are like sword thrusts, but the tongue of the wise brings healing." Proverbs 12:18 (ESV)

"A gentle tongue is a tree of life, but perverseness in it breaks the spirit." Proverbs 15:4 (ESV)

"But no human being can tame the tongue. It is a restless evil, full of deadly poison." James 3:8 (NIV)

"Death and life are in the power of the tongue, and those who love it will eat its fruits." Proverbs 18:21 (ESV)

"Whoever keeps his mouth and his tongue, keeps himself out of trouble." Proverbs 21:23 (ESV)

"I tell you, on the day of judgment people will give account for every careless word they speak, for by your words you will be justified, and by your words you will be condemned." Matthew 12:36–37 (ESV)

I once read this profound statement by Mary Southerland on her Girlfriends in God blog—"Godly responses come from the heart. If there is something wrong with our words, then there is something wrong with our heart." Wow! That cuts to the core. All we have to do is re-read Proverbs 16:23 to recognize the truth in this statement. The words we say are a direct reflection of the health of our heart. Luke 6:45 (ESV) says, *"The good person out of the good treasure of his heart produces good, and the evil person out of his evil treasure produces evil, for out of the abundance of the heart his mouth speaks."*

We must pray that when we speak, our words will reflect a heart of love; a heart that loves God and desires to honor Him each and every day. Let's throw away the sticks and stones and only speak words that follow the advice from Ephesians 4:29 (ESV): *"Let no corrupting talk come out of your mouths, but only such as is good for building up, as fits the occasion, that it may give grace to those who hear."* ❧

19

Give Thanks

"Give thanks to the Lord, for He is good; His love endures forever."

PSALM 107:1 (NIV)

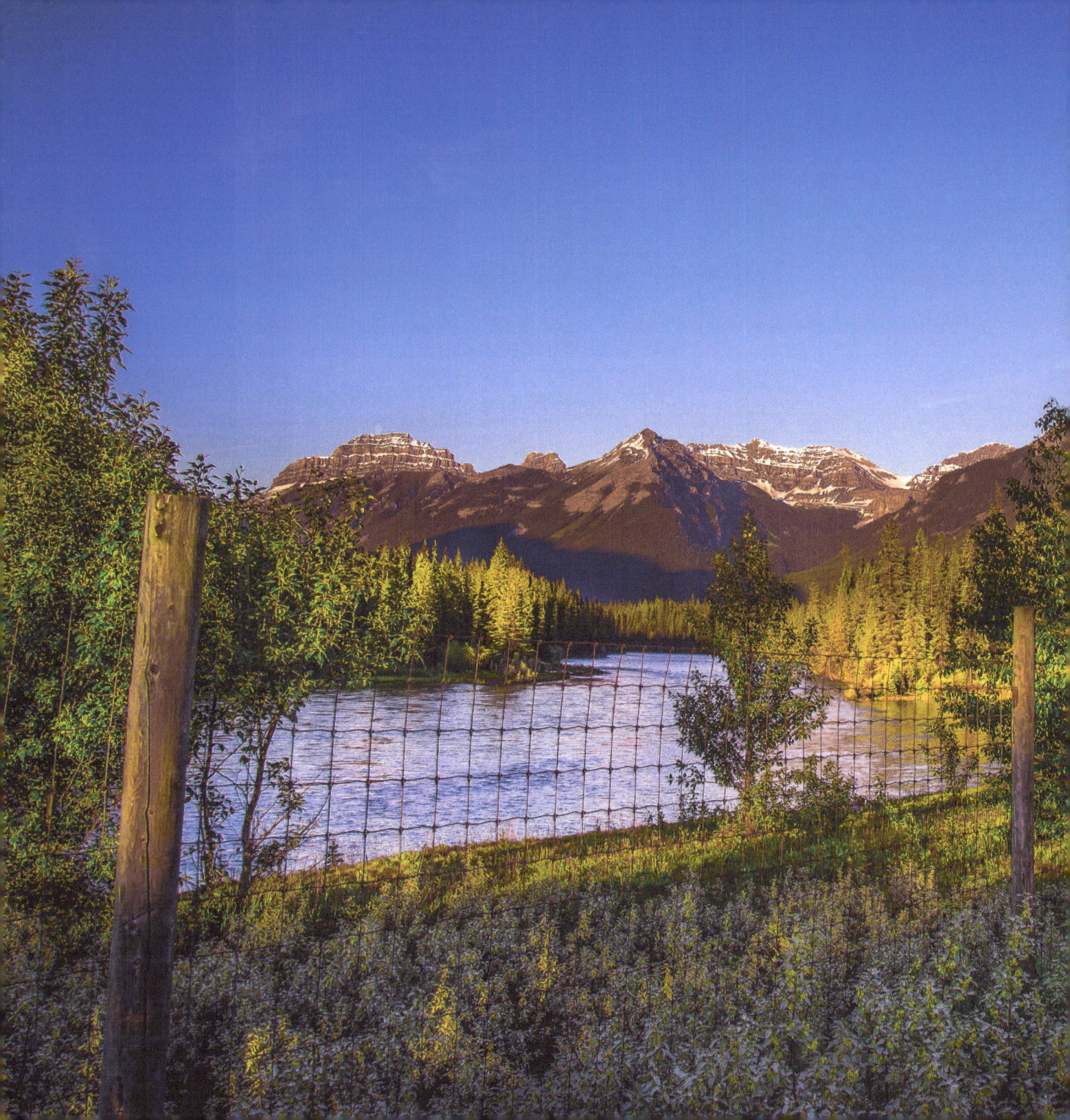

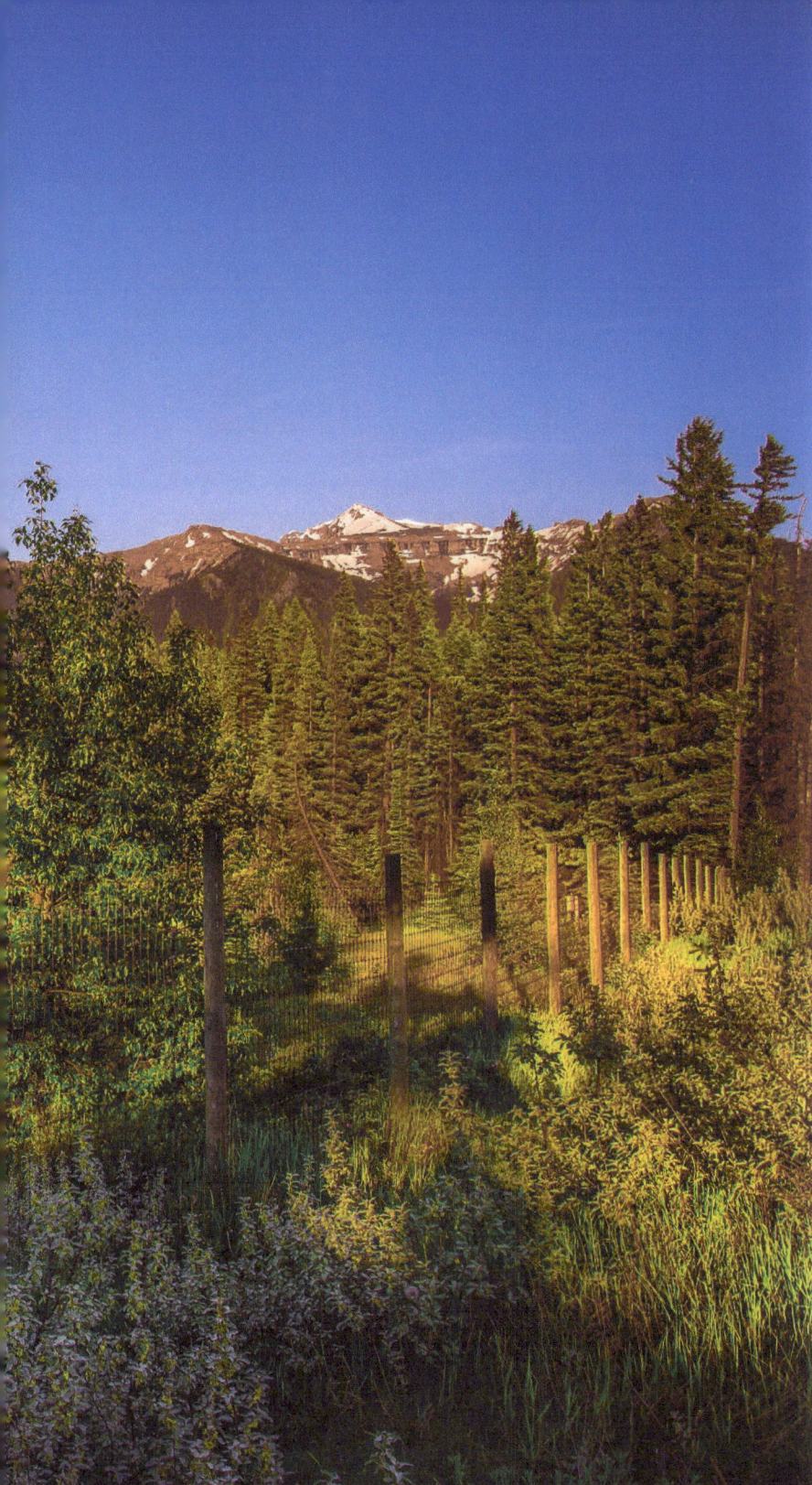

Each year on the fourth Thursday of November, Americans celebrate the Thanksgiving holiday.

It is a day set aside to give thanks for the blessing of the harvest of the preceding year. There is some debate about the details of the first Thanksgiving celebrations, but one fact remains: for many years people have offered prayers of thanks and held special ceremonies of thanksgiving after bringing in the harvest. They recognize the blessings of abundance, and celebrating those blessings is a way of expressing gratitude.

Merriam-Webster defines *thanks* as "a good feeling that you have towards someone who has helped you." Gratitude is defined as "a feeling of thanks and appreciation." Both definitions include the word *feeling*. Thankfulness is a feeling; gratitude is a *feeling*. One cannot be thankful without the feeling that accompanies it. That feeling of thankfulness and gratitude, in turn, has

OTHER SIDE OF THE FENCE,
BANFF NATIONAL PARK,
ALBERTA, CANADA

a definite effect on one's attitude.

William Arthur Ward once said, "Gratitude can transform common days into thanksgivings, turn routine jobs into joy, and change ordinary opportunities into blessings." Each of those things mentioned in Ward's quote has everything to do with the attitude. When we begin to count our blessings and thank God for them, our attitude toward other things begins to change as well. As we recognize the source of our blessings—God—and begin to thank Him, we begin to develop an attitude of gratitude.

Having an attitude of gratitude means we must make it a habit to express thankfulness and appreciation in all parts of our lives. As Oprah Winfrey once said, "Be thankful for what you have; you'll end up having more. If you concentrate on what you don't have, you will never, ever have enough.

Unfortunately, too many of us take our blessings for granted. We fail to be thankful for the things we have. Satan wants us to think that there must be something more out there for us—that this can't be all there is. We look at the grass on the other side of the fence and see it as something better than what we already have. That is a dangerous line of thinking. An attitude of ingratitude only yields pain and disappointment. The Bible is filled with incidents of ingratitude to God for His gifts. In each incident, ingratitude ushered in suffering and punishment.

Give thanks to God for the blessings He bestows. God knows what is best for us. He knows exactly what we need and don't need. He sees a much bigger picture than our shielded eyes can see. He loves us. He promises to take care of us. Be thankful in all things. *"Give thanks to the Lord, for He is good; His love endures forever."*

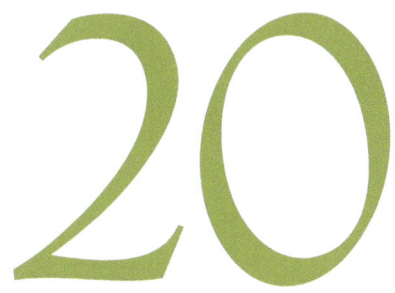

20

Flawless

"For all have sinned and come short of the glory of God."

ROMANS 3:23 (NIV)

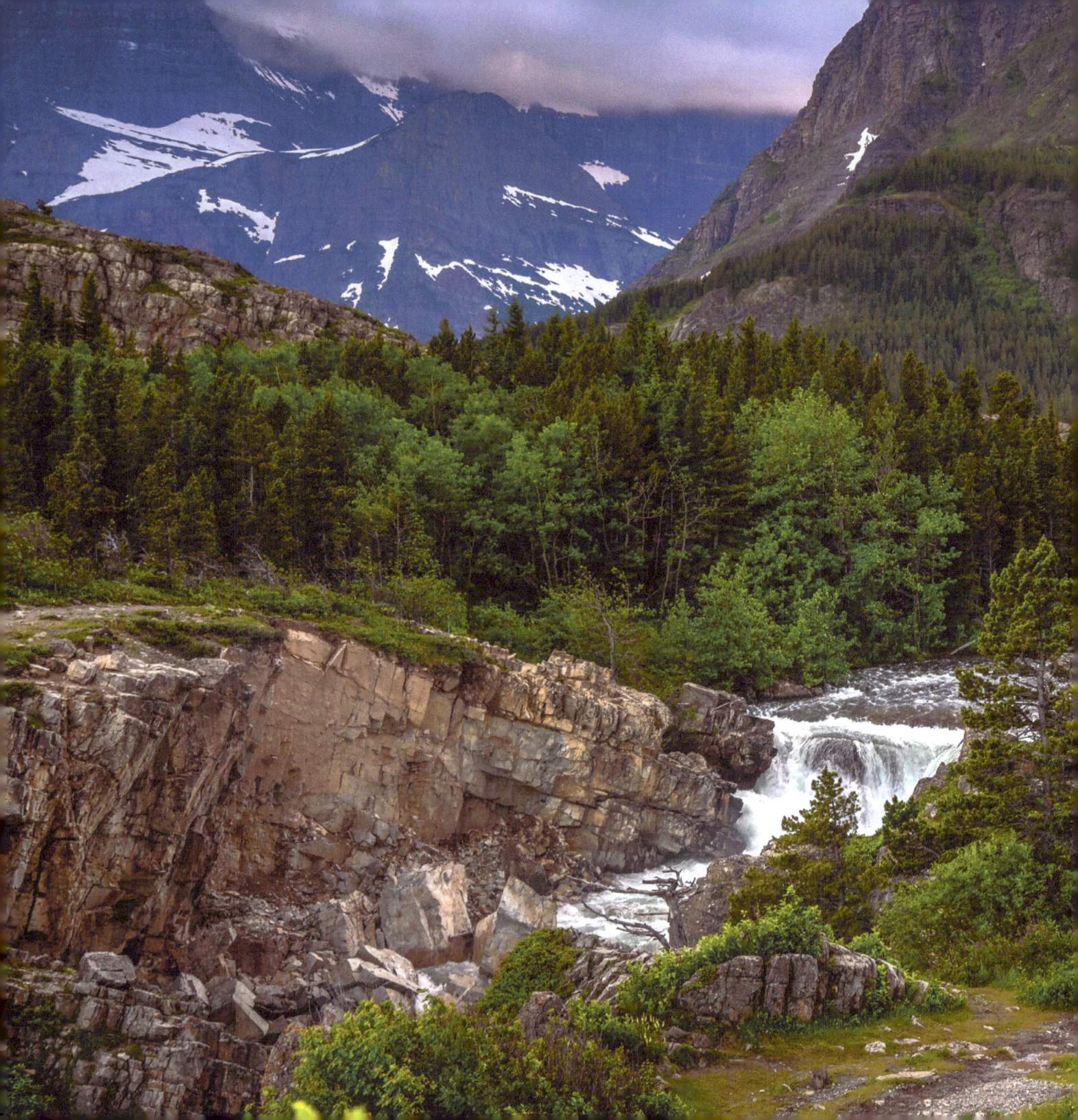

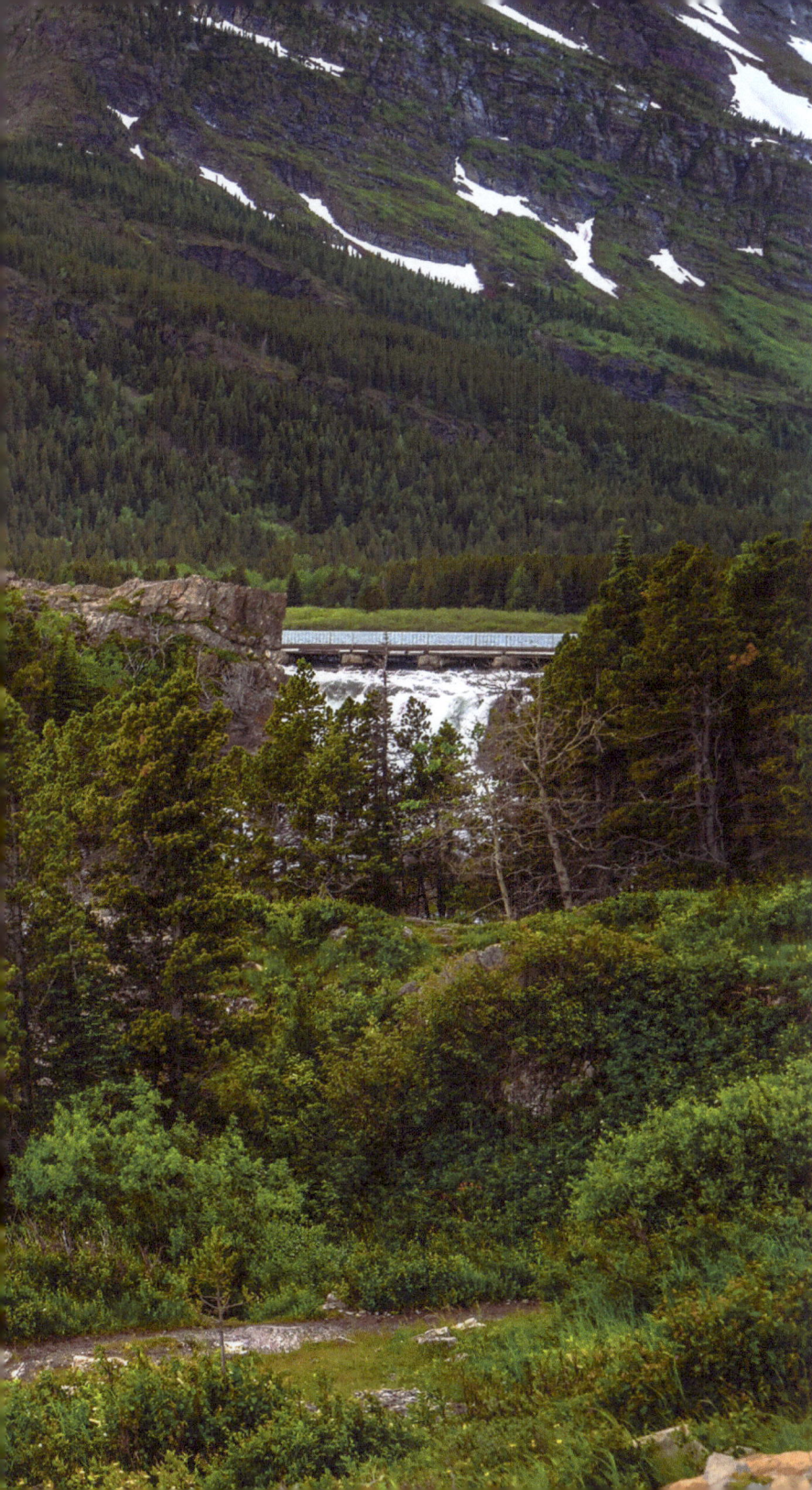

Nature is amazing.

It is impossible to look around and not see the beauty in all of creation. The birds, the bees, the flowers, the mountains, the streams, all of it is beautiful in its own flawless way. Human beings are part of nature, too, but do we see humanity in the same way? Flawless: "without any blemishes or imperfections; perfect; without any mistakes or shortcomings." Can anyone ever fit that definition? It's not likely.

Too often people think that they have to wait to fix their problems before God will love and accept them. They think that the error of their ways is too horrible for God to forgive them; that their sin runs too deep to ever warrant the love of God. However, the exact opposite is true. It is when we are dirty, when we are at our lowest point, when we are in a desperate state of need that God reaches down and pulls us out of the mire.

In Luke 15, Jesus illustrated the magnitude of God's love through the story of the prodigal son. In this story, a father gave his young son the portion of his wealth that was due to him. Out of the ignorance of his youth, the young man squandered away his portion with riotous living. Soon he found himself in a nasty situation. A famine spread throughout the land, he was out of money,

GLACIER NATIONAL PARK, MONTANA

and the young man found himself in dire need. He took a job as a swine handler, and he found that he was so hungry that he longed to eat the husks offered to the swine. At the lowest point of desperation, the young son decided to head back to his father's land and beg his father to hire him as a servant. He feared that his father would reject him, yet he knew he had no other options. While he was still far off, the young man's father recognized his son, and ran to him. The son braced himself for the worst; however, his father embraced him and ordered that the fatted calf be prepared for a celebration. His son, whom he feared he had lost, had finally returned.

That's how Jesus looks at us. He sees us when we are at our lowest point, yet He loves us unconditionally like the father of the prodigal son. Jesus takes us as we are—low, dirty, flawed—and loves us anyway.

Romans 3:23 declares that all of us have a sinful nature. We all fail at one time or another. Not one of us is flawless. But that's not the final truth. When Christ died on the cross, He represented us and took our sins to the cross with Him. His death wiped away our sin and made it possible for us to have a relationship with God, our Father. The cross has made us flawless. Flawless: "without any blemishes or imperfections; perfect; without any mistakes or shortcomings." That is who we are in Christ. ଔ

21

What's in a Name

"The angel said to her, 'Do not be afraid, Mary; for you have found favor with God. And behold, you will conceive in your womb and bear a son, and you shall name Him Jesus.'"

LUKE 1:31 (NASB)

"She will bear a son, and you shall call his name Jesus, for he will save his people from their sins."

MATTHEW 1:21 (ESV)

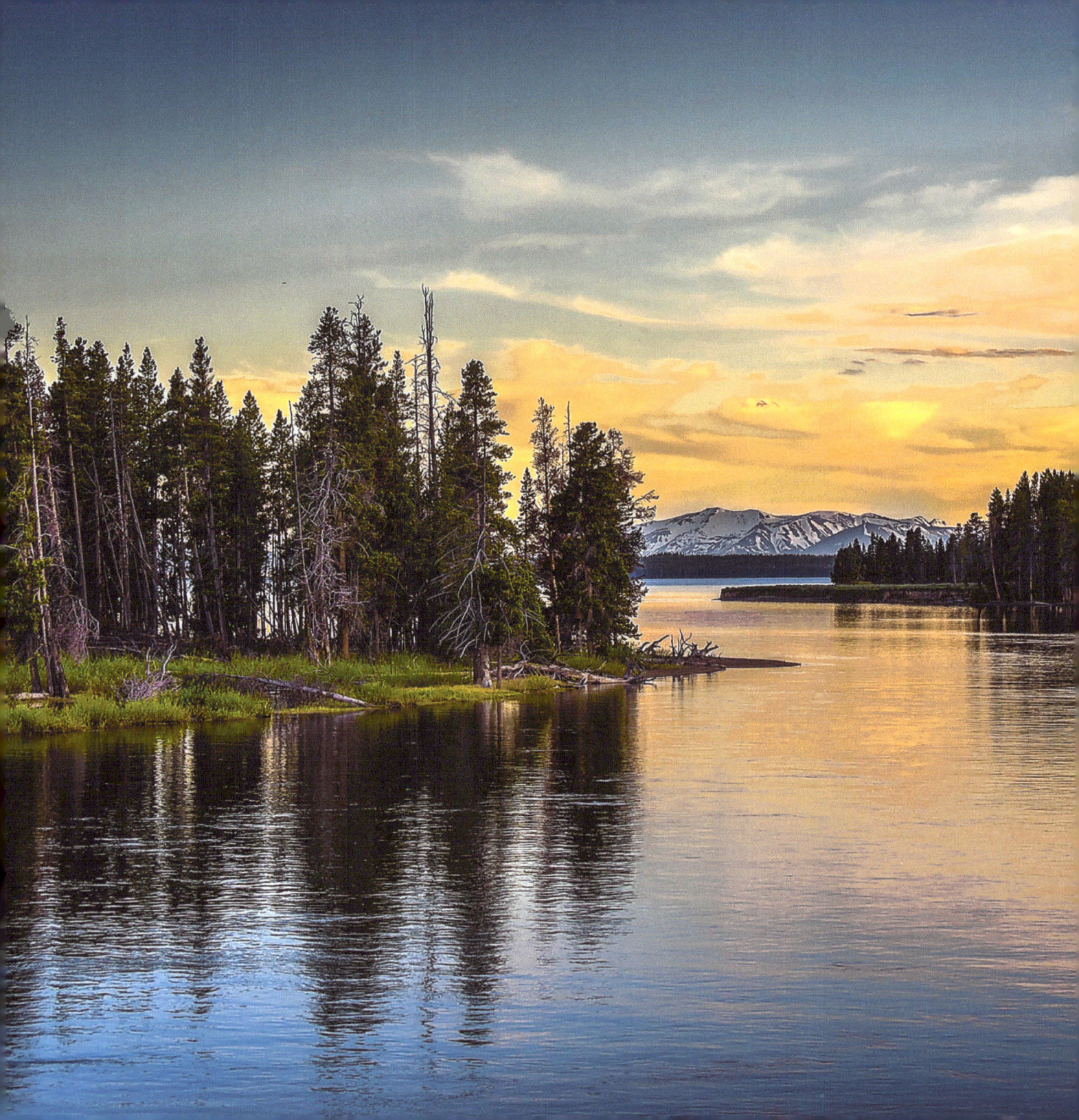

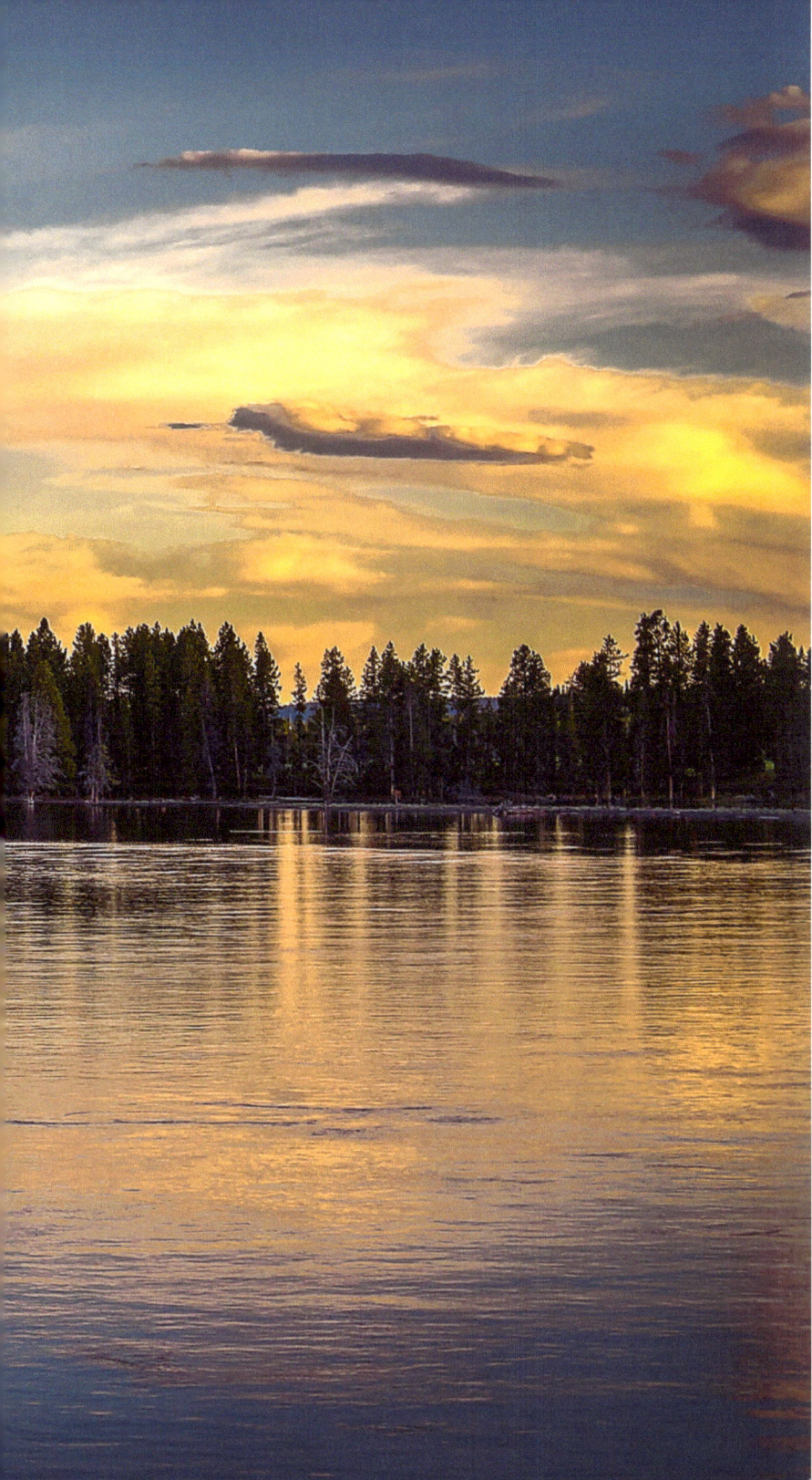

I have taught at the middle school level for quite a number of years, and in that time I've learned that knowing my students' names is crucial to success- fully managing my classroom.

The sooner I learn their names, the sooner I can relate to them and they to me. There is something powerful in knowing that someone cares enough to call you by name. For centuries names have held power and value. Names are immortalized in poetry, in all forms of writing, and in religious ceremonies. Everyone recognizes himself or herself by name.

When the angel appeared to Mary with the news that she would conceive a child, a son, the very Son of God, the angel gave her explicit instructions regarding

YELLOWSTONE LAKE, YELLOWSTONE NATIONAL PARK, WYOMING

what to name the child. A short time later, an angel appeared to Joseph in a dream and told him to take Mary as his wife and that she would give birth to a son who was to be named Jesus.

The name Jesus means "Savior." This is His special role. Jesus was sent down from heaven by God the Father to free us all from the guilt of sin by cleansing us in His own atoning blood. He saved us from the clutches of sin by offering Himself in our place on the cross. In the days to come, He provides a way to save us from the presence of sin when He takes us out of this world to rest with Him. He truly is our Savior!

The name Jesus is a very encouraging name to those heavy burdened by sin. He is the King of kings and the Lord of lords. Other savior-leaders in history have taken more high-sounding titles like "the Great" or "the Conqueror," but that kind of glory was not what Jesus was seeking for Himself. The Son of God didn't need a fancy name to make Himself great. He was content to call Himself "Savior." He knew who He was and what His purpose was. He came to Earth for us. He is our salvation.

Our salvation has a name! Jesus! He came as flesh and blood and walked on the same earth we do. He lived and grew as each of us did. He experienced love, fear, pain, and rejection just like each of us. The Son of God lived life as a mortal, and in so doing, made a way for us to commune with God the Father.

There is power in the name of Jesus. When you don't know what words to say, just say "Jesus." Trust Him. He'll see you through. What's in a name? Power. Rest. Peace. Hope. Jesus! Savior! Praise His Holy Name! ଔ

22

Let It Rain

"So let us know, let us press on to know the Lord. His going forth is as certain as the dawn; And He will come to us like the rain, like the spring rain watering the earth."

HOSEA 6:3 (NASB)

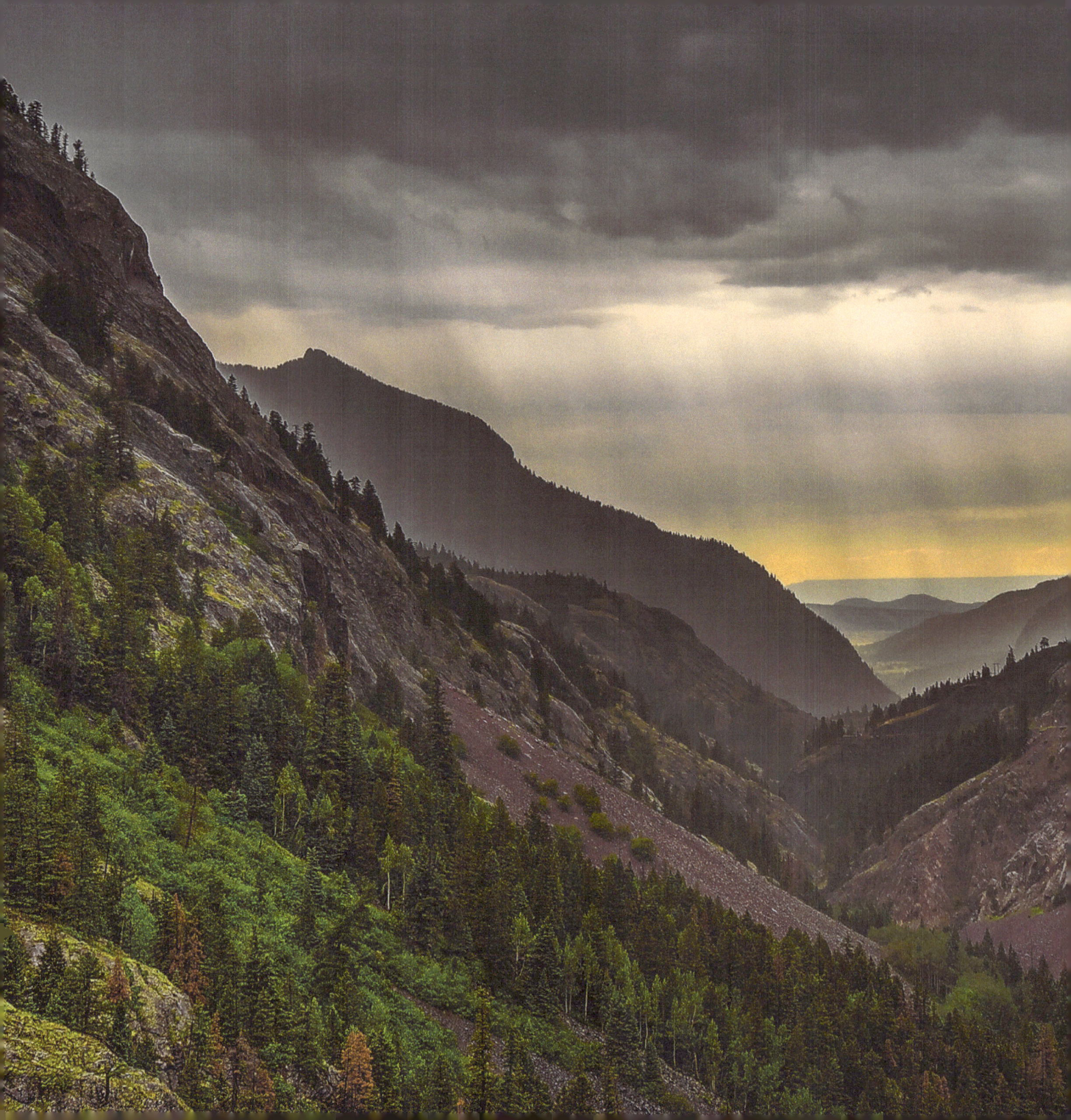

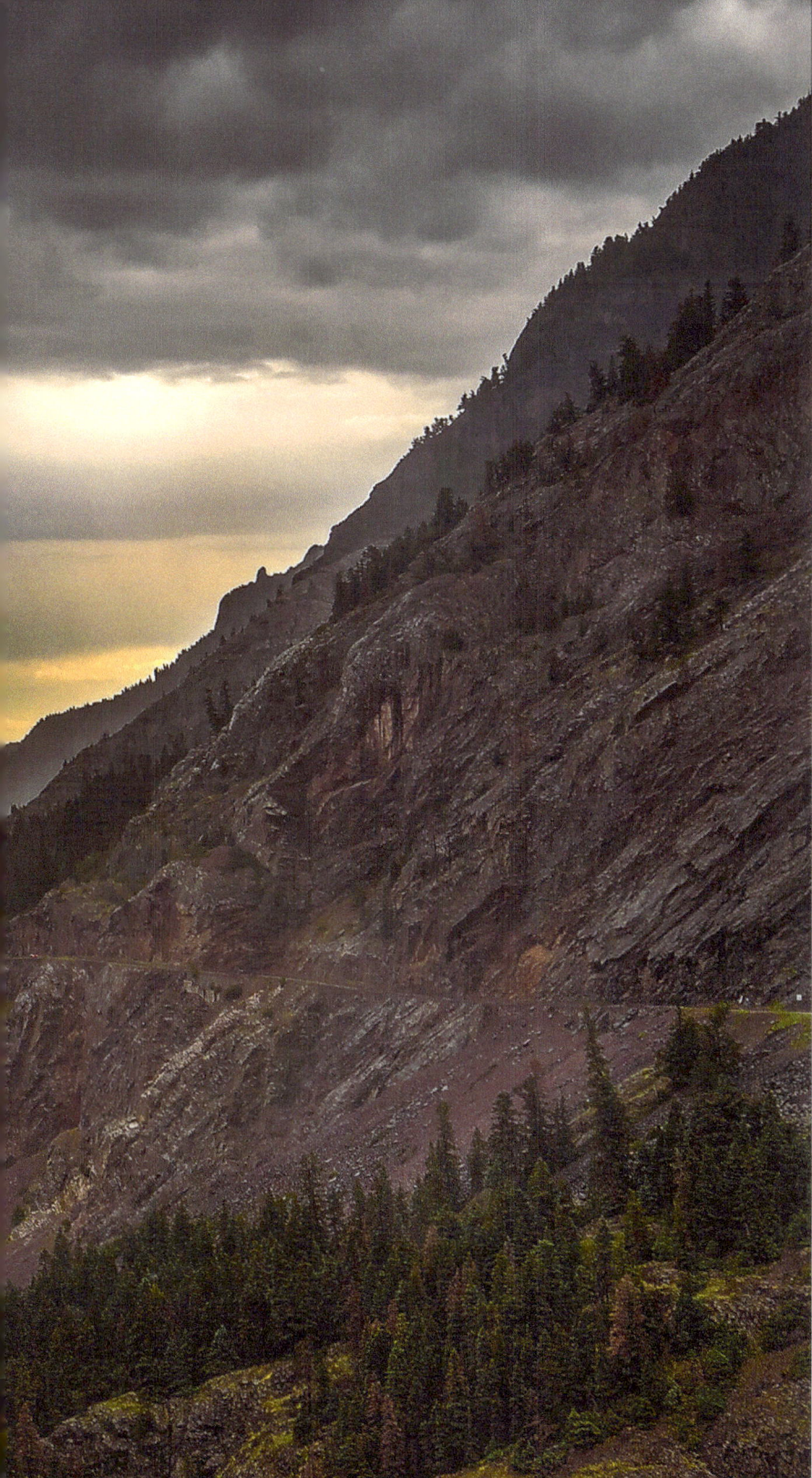

Rain. Drops of liquid that gather in the heavens above and fall to the earth below.

No one on earth can control it. It falls when it has gathered enough of itself to succumb to the pull of gravity.

We may not like rain when it spoils our plans or brings a sense of gloom to our souls, but without rain, all of earth feels the effect. The grass shrivels up and turns brown. The earth withdraws within itself and opens up cracks of thirst. The animals wander in search of replenishing water. Everything gathers a layer of dust and filth.

When the rain falls though, it brings a cleansing, replenishing freshness. It quenches the thirst of the land and nourishes the animals. The grass turns greener and the trees turn brighter. It feeds the rivers and streams, and it washes away the remnants of drier times. All life on earth is dependent upon the power of rain.

Our souls are no different. We need the refreshing rain poured down on us as we grow and flourish in our knowledge of the Lord. The only way to know more

MILLION DOLLAR HIGHWAY,
US ROUTE 550, OURAY,
COLORADO

of God is to spend more time with Him. Like the rain-drops that gather together in the heavens before falling down from above, we need to know more of Him so that He can pour out from our lives. When we spend time with Him, we allow more of Him to fill us. We become more like Him. Then, and only then, can we become effective witnesses for Him. In 2 Timothy 3:16–17 (ESV) we read, *"All scripture is breathed out by God and profitable for teaching, for reproof, for* *correction, and for training in righteousness, that the man of God may be complete, equipped for every good work."* As we draw closer to God, His word becomes clearer to us and we find ourselves better equipped to lead others to the throne.

The more time we spend with Him, the more attuned we become to His mighty greatness, and the more His power will rain down on us—cleansing us; replenishing us; renewing us. Let it rain! ‿

23

Be Still

"Be still, and know that I am God."

PSALM 46:10 (ESV)

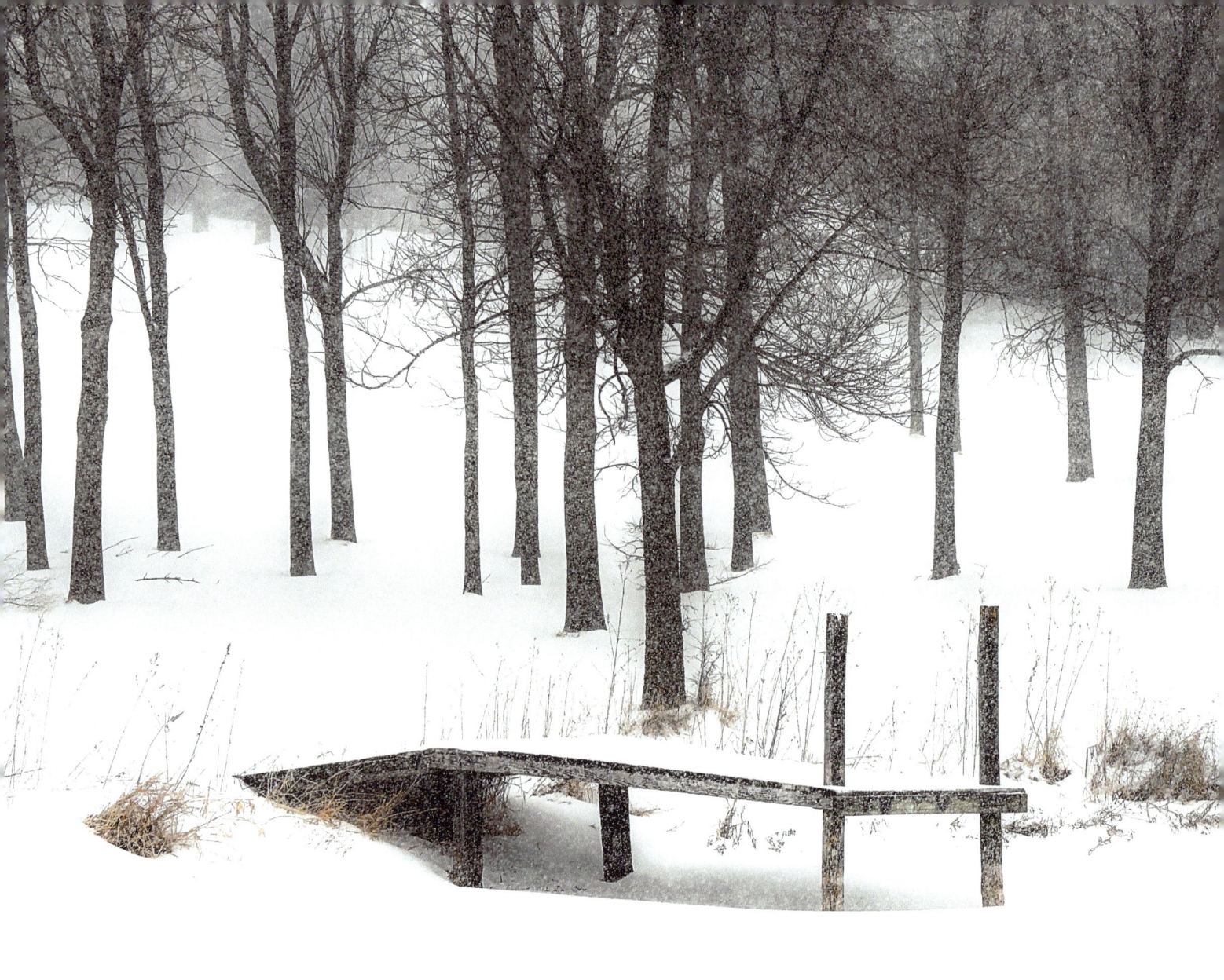

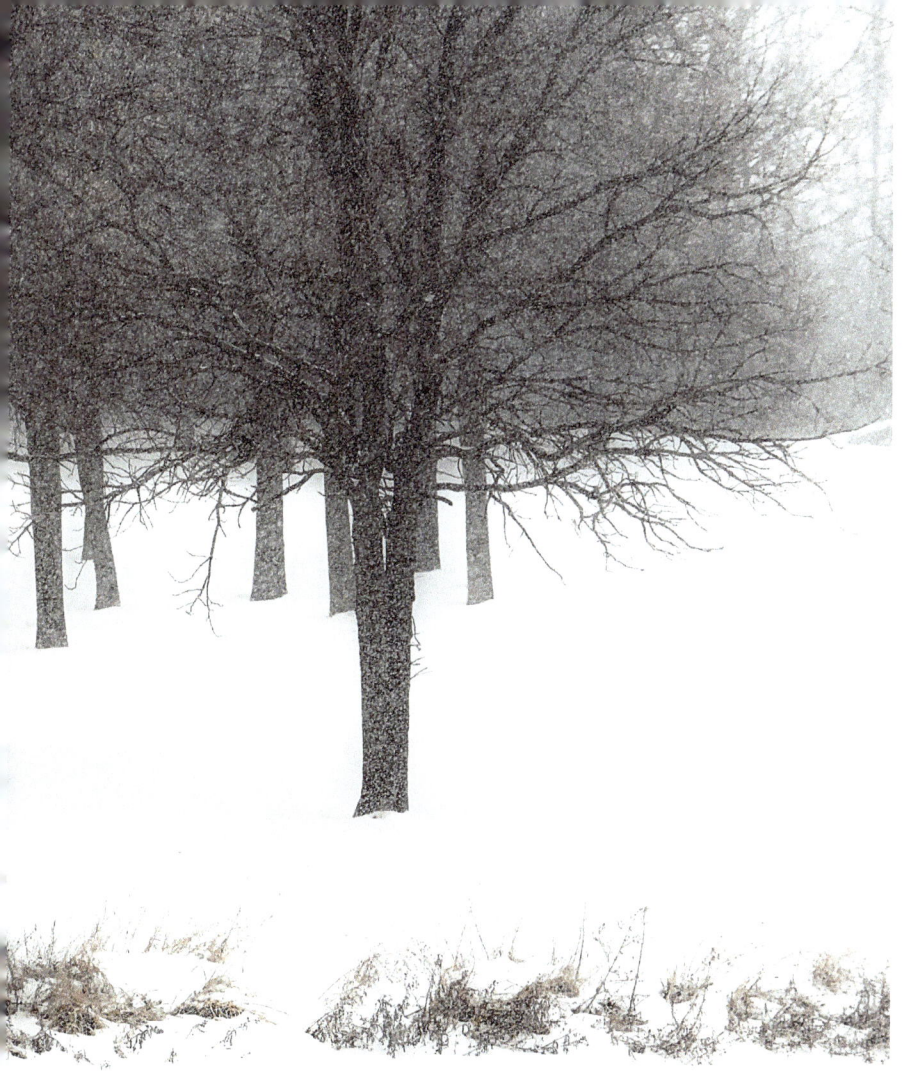

It is easy to get caught up in the hustle and bustle of everyday life.

This is especially true during the Christmas holiday. At a time when people should be spending time enjoying the sights and sounds that accompany the celebration of the birth of Christ, many find it anything but peaceful. This is a time when stress seems to multiply by leaps and bounds. There are gifts to buy, cookies to bake, parties to attend, gifts to wrap, and people to visit. Sometimes there is so much going on that we forget about the real reason we celebrate Christmas.

Recently I saw a painting of an artist's interpretation of what the birth of Jesus might have looked like before the shepherds arrived and the excitement surrounding the arrival of the long-awaited king ensued. The painting depicted a tiny baby, swaddled tightly and lying on a bed of straw, a weary Mary slumped in exhaustion against the wooden manger, and Joseph stooping over the manger, leaning on his shepherd's staff with a look of fatigue etched on his face. Most of us don't usually think about the birth of Christ

FARM POND IN WINTER,
OSKALOOSA, IOWA

in that manner of humanness. We tend to envision the tranquil, ethereal scene often printed on Christmas cards. The scene of the painting is the exact opposite, but it paints a more accurate picture of what truly happened.

Tranquility is not often the atmosphere that surrounds moments following the birth of a child, but every new mother and father need it. Mary and Joseph were no different. God did not send the angels to the shepherds right away. He gave the new parents the chance for some peace and quiet, some time to be alone with their newborn child before all of the excitement began.

All of us need a period of quietness to still our troubled, weary souls. The verses that come before Psalm 46:10 tell of destruction, fire, and calamity, not peace and tranquility. We need to find that place where, regardless of the trials that came before, we can find rest and renewal. It is during those times of trial that we need to be still and find peace. It doesn't matter what battles we have fought, what fires we have walked through, what calamity has befallen us, we must find time to be still.

God knew that we would need rest, so He admonishes us to be still, to rest, to seek peace. He reminds us that He is with us in all things. He will not leave us nor forsake us. He is the Alpha and the Omega, the beginning and the end.

Be still. Rest in who He is. And know that He is God through it all. ଔ

24

Through the Looking Glass

"For where your treasure is, there
will your heart be also."

MATTHEW 6:21 (NIV)

"As water reflects the face, so one's
life reflects the heart."

PROVERBS 27:19 (NIV)

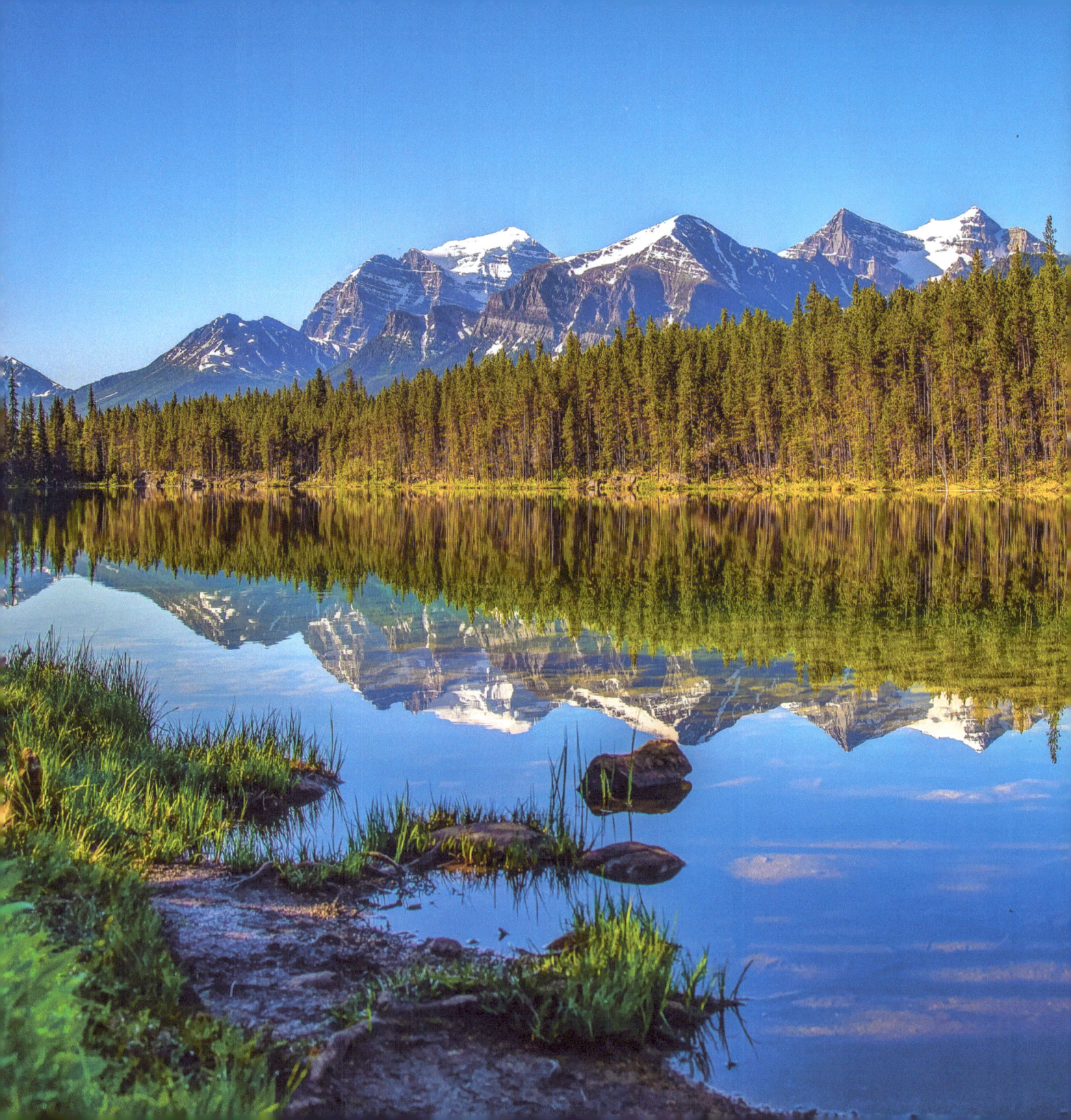

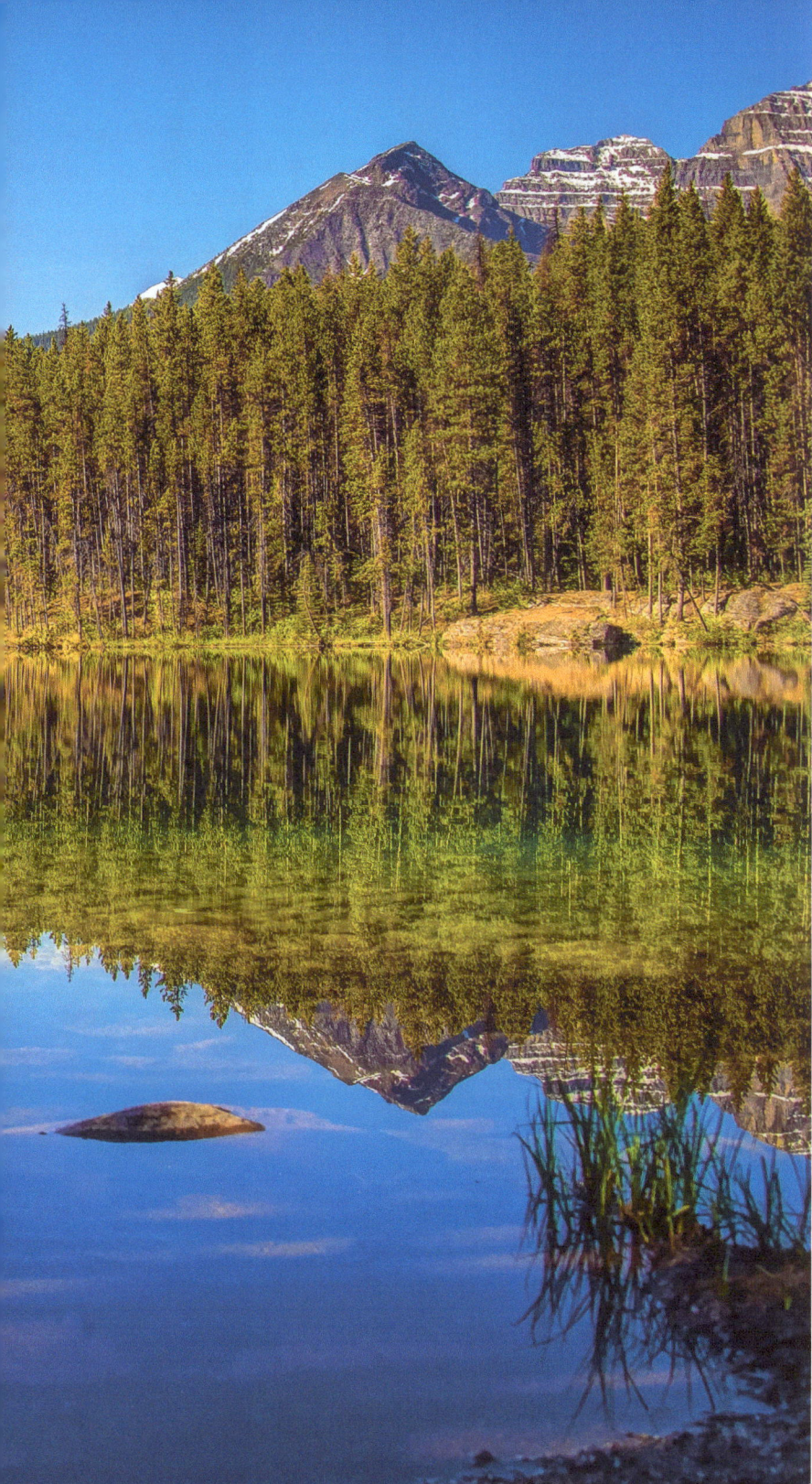

They say that pictures do not lie.

Neither do mirrors, reflections, and small children. Pictures and mirrors that have not been altered in some form or another show truth. Reflections show truth, albeit a somewhat distorted truth. Small children, on the other hand, are blatantly honest. Just ask one his opinion, and he'll tell you how it is. All of these things provide an honest look at our outward appearances regardless of our willingness to accept that truth. We may not like what we see, but sometimes we need to look at ourselves through one of those avenues just to get a better picture of who we really are on the outside.

But looks can be deceiving. What appears on the outside is not always the honest truth on the inside. It doesn't take long to suddenly begin to see what truly lies within. This fact is rather unfortunate and happens all too often.

It only takes seven seconds to make a strong first impression. One chance. Seven seconds. That's it. Unfortunately, even first impressions—gut feelings—can be wrong. Too often we discover that our first impressions are slightly jaded. The more time we spend with someone, the more his inner self begins

MIRROR LAKE, BANFF
NATIONAL PARK, ALBERTA,
CANADA

to surface. And vice versa.

So, what impression are we giving? Is it accurate? Does it really reveal our inner heart? What makes us tick? Who are we? Are we the same when things get rough? How do we handle ourselves under stress? What traits are revealed when things don't go the way we want? What drives us? Who are we when no one is looking? These are all good questions we need to ponder.

Proverbs 27:19 tells us that our life reflects that which is in our heart, and Matthew 6:21 reminds us that our heart reveals those things that we treasure. Periodically we need to do a heart inventory. By looking at those things that consume our time, our attention, and our finances, we get a glimpse into the reality of our heart.

Matthew 6:19-20 (NIV) gives instruction regarding matters of the heart. *"Do not store up for yourselves treasures on earth, where moths and vermin destroy, and where thieves break in and steal. But store up for yourselves treasures in heaven, where moths and vermin do not destroy, and where thieves do not break in and steal."* The things of this earth are not eternal and are of little value when compared to the heavenly realm; therefore we shouldn't put so much emphasis on them. In today's world, that is easier said than done, but not impossible.

The Bible tells us that all things are possible through Christ if we just believe. When we ask Christ to reveal our true, inner selves, we can become more like Him. When we take time to pray and commune with our Heavenly Father, He reveals those areas within that need work. With His help, we can have a complete heart inventory, and we can change those areas that are more worldly and less than heavenly. When we pray, we need to ask God to help us look beyond the outer image in the looking glass and begin to see what's on the other side, on the inside.

God wants nothing more for us than the very best. He wants us to become more like Him. When we allow ourselves to become vulnerable to the truth, and then allow Him to work in and through us, we become all He wants us to be; we become all He created us to be. ⍵

25

Light of the World

"The true light that gives light to everyone was coming into the world. He was in the world, and though the world was made through him, the world did not recognize him. He came to that which was his own, but his own did not receive him. Yet to all who did receive him, to those who believed in his name, he gave the right to become children of God—children born not of natural descent, nor of human decision or a husband's will, but born of God. The Word became flesh and made his dwelling among us. We have seen his glory, the glory of the one and only Son, who came from the Father, full of grace and truth."

JOHN 1:9–14 (NIV)

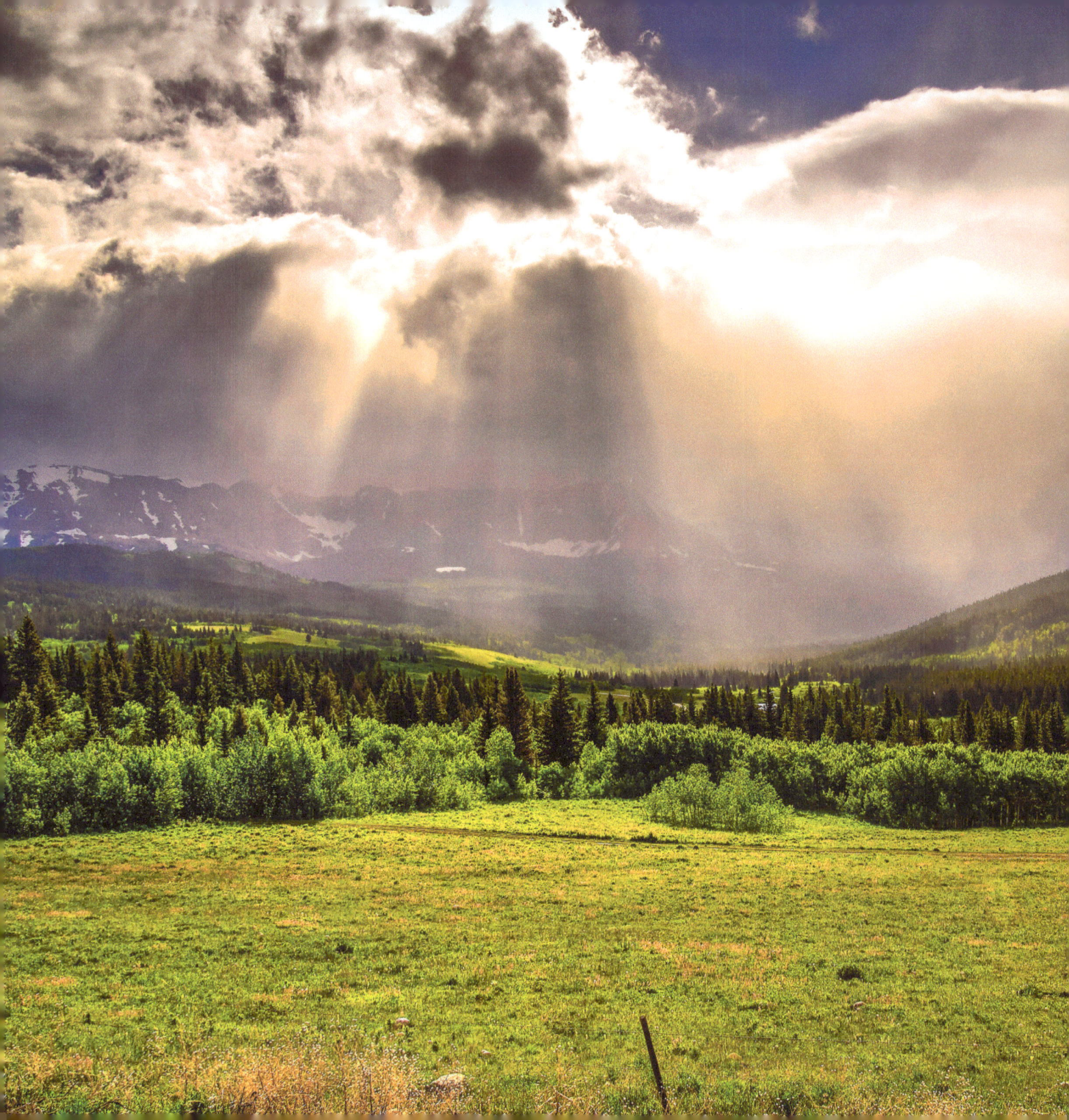

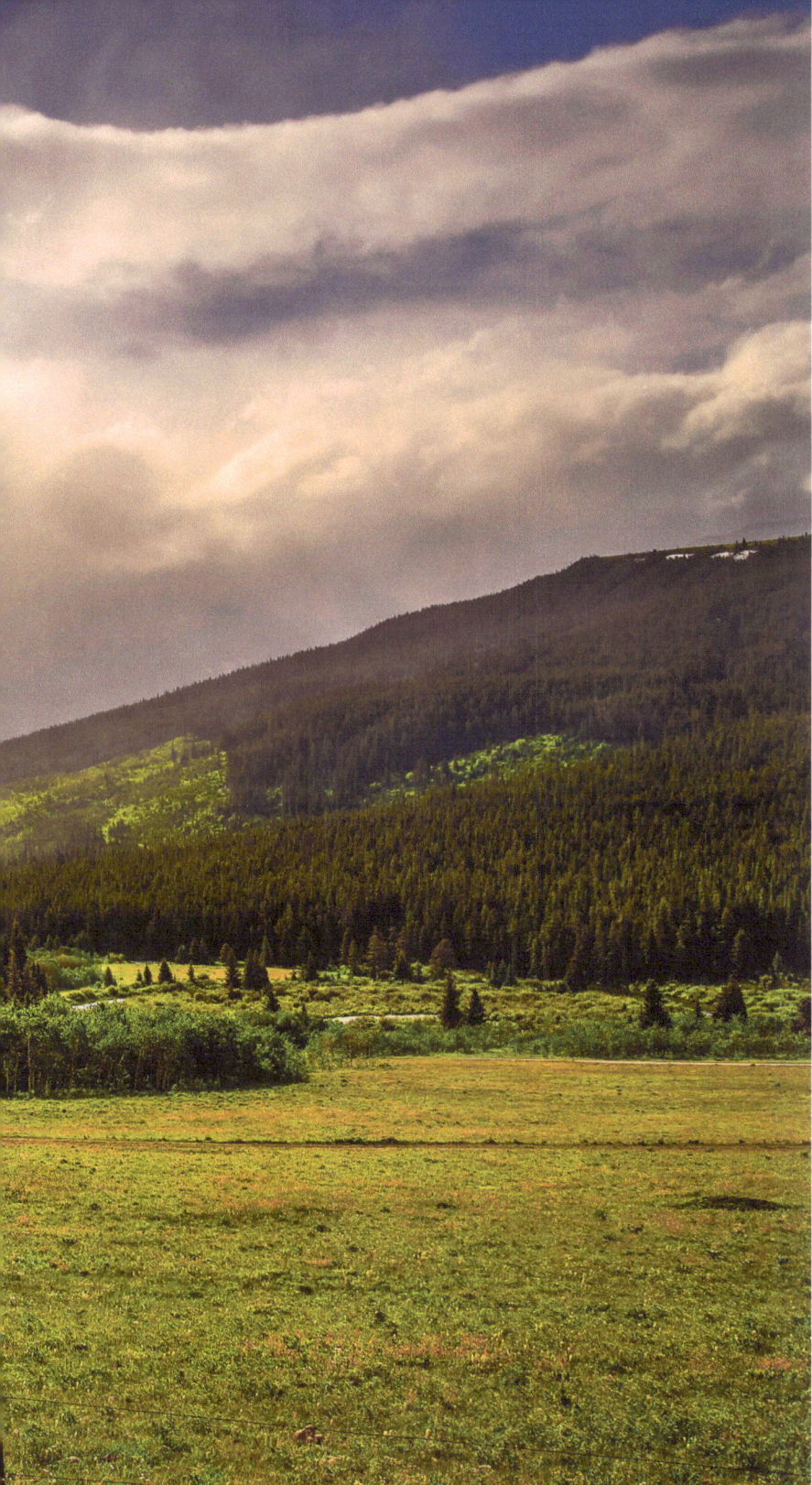

Light. Luminous energy. Radiant energy.

Electromagnetic radiation, which causes the organs of sight to react. All of these definitions are scientific, but even though the definitions are accurate, they don't make it easier to understand the true meaning of the word. In simpler terms, light makes things visible.

The word "light" in John 1 isn't talking about an actual light, a beacon of luminous energy that allows things to be seen. In this verse, the word light is referring to Jesus Christ, the light of the world. *". . . Jesus spoke to them, saying, 'I am the light of the world. Whoever follows me will not walk in darkness, but will have the light of life'"* (John 8:12, ESV). When Jesus refers to Himself as "the light of the world," He is referring to the contrast of light to darkness. Good versus evil. In the same way that light removes darkness, Jesus came to earth to save us from a life of evil, a life of sin.

Jesus came to us as a baby. A tiny, innocent little baby. A perfect, flawless baby. No one expected the savior to come in such a manner. The Jews had their own idea how their king would come, but a

BREAKING THROUGH,
GLACIER NATIONAL PARK,
MONTANA

baby definitely was not what they had envisioned. They expected their savior to usher in a whole new world, wipe out their oppressors, and rule the world according to Jewish standards. They were looking for a king that fit their vision, their expectations. God, however, had a different vision.

Each of us was born with a free will. Proverbs 16:9 (ESV) says, *"The heart of man plans his way, but the Lord establishes his steps."* We are all given full control of our thoughts, our choices, our decisions. Yes, there are consequences for those choices, but the ultimate decisions come from within. To save us, God sent His only Son to earth to live among man, to die a cruel death on a cross. God loved us so much that He made the ultimate sacrifice so that we could have hope for eternal life with Him. He has laid out a path for us. He provides guidance and wisdom. But He does not choose for us. *"Behold, I stand at the door and knock. If anyone hears my voice and opens the door, I will come in to him and eat with him, and he with me"* (Revelation 3:20, ESV). The opportunity is there for us to receive light. But the choice is ours to make.

Jesus came to bring light. But that light is not *given* to everyone. It is *created* for everyone; it is available to everyone; it is *offered* to everyone; but it is only given to those who receive it. *"Whoever follows me will not walk in darkness, but will have the light of life."* Can receiving the light of life be as simple as merely believing? Absolutely! Claim the light! Believe! Receive the light of the world! And see for the very first time! ೞ

26

Stuff Happens

"I can do all things through Christ who strengthens me."

PHILIPPIANS 4:13 (NKJV)

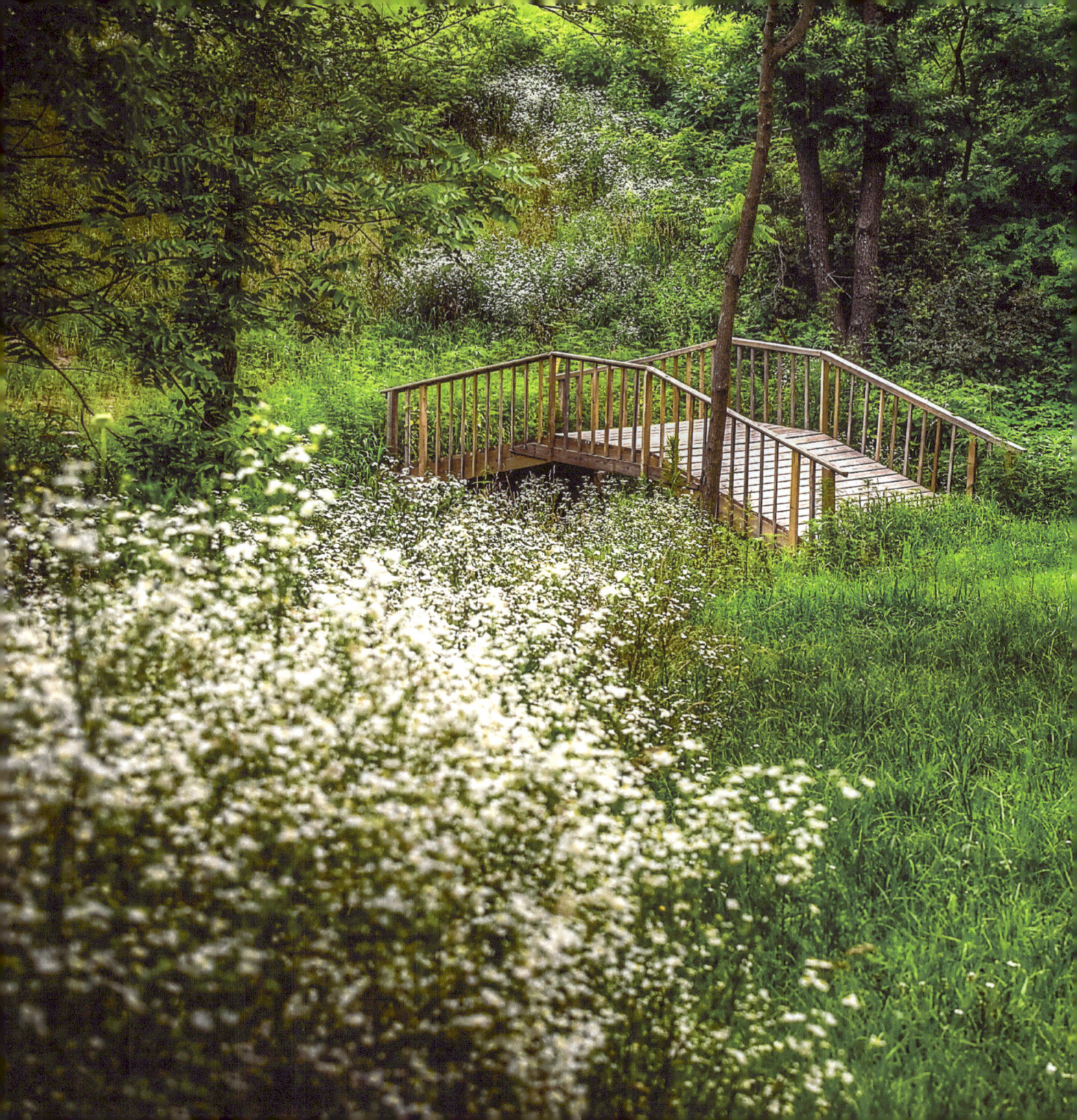

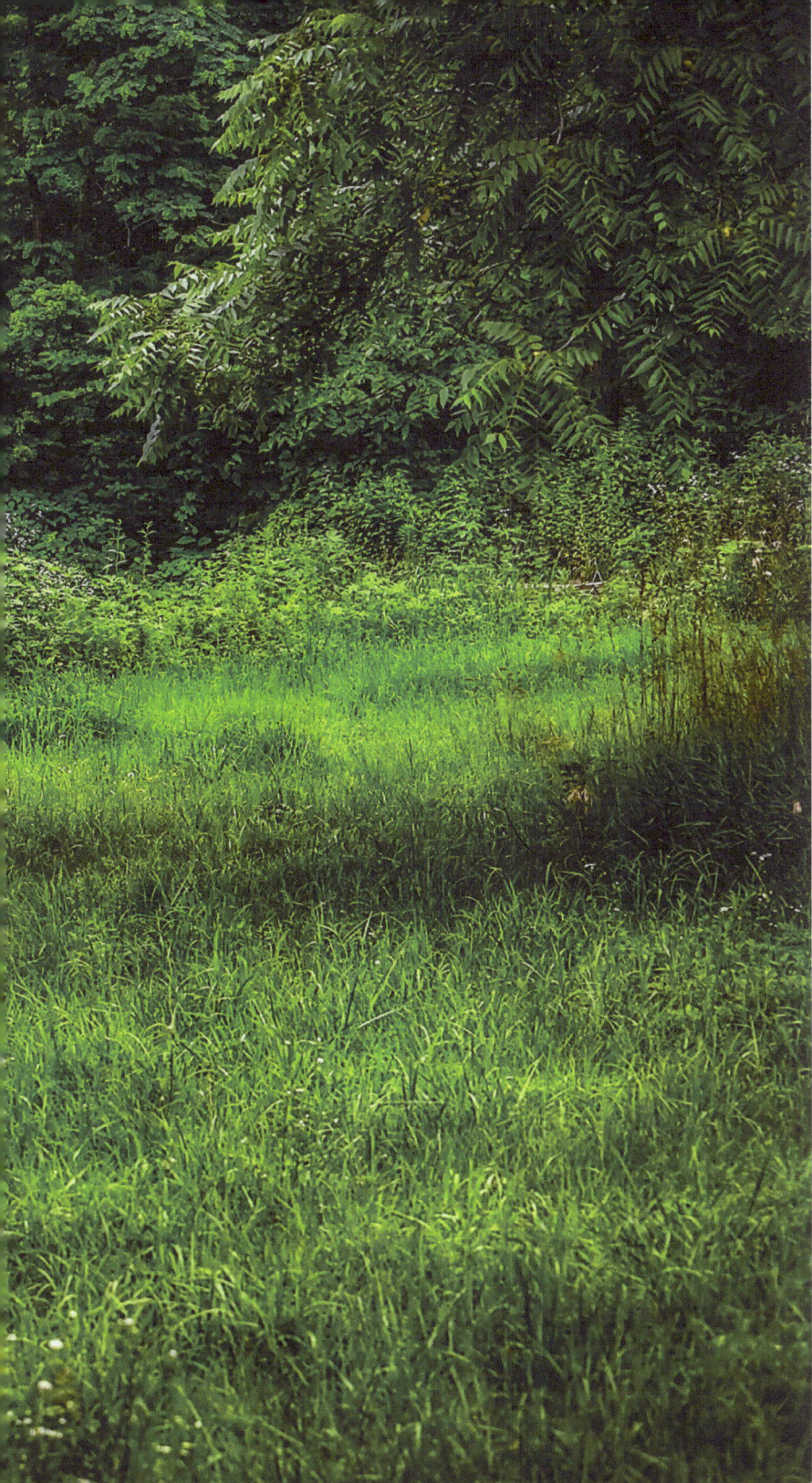

At some point in our lives we will all face hardship.

It may come as the death of a loved one, the loss of a job, a devastating fire, the diagnosis of cancer, or the burden of financial struggle. Hardship has many faces and can be unbearably relentless. We've all heard the phrase "When it rains it pours." Unfortunately, that statement rings true more often than not.

These are the times when we ask ourselves the rhetorical questions: When will it end? Why me? How much more can I take? We ask these questions not really expecting an answer. Often times there is no answer. Things just happen.

It isn't uncommon for life to throw an occasional curveball in our direction. We don't know when or how that curveball will come in, but we know it will come sooner or later. And I guarantee it won't be fair. Stuff happens. Someone once said, "If you aren't experiencing hardship now, just wait. It's comin'. " We hope that isn't true, but in our heart of hearts, we know it is. It's just a matter of time. So what do we do when that day arrives? Well, we have three options. We can choose to let the hardship destroy us.

BRIDGE TO NOWHERE,
OSKALOOSA, IOWA

We can choose to let it define us. Or we can choose to let it strengthen us. The ball is in our court. We may not like the circumstances under which that ball came, but it is in our court. Now what are we going to do with it?

It seems like a no-brainer that people would choose to let their hardships strengthen them, but unfortunately not everyone makes this choice. Each choice yields a set of characteristics that are easy to identify.

Who are the people who choose to let hardship destroy them? These are the people who have no hope. They have lost sight of the promises of God or, sadly, didn't ever believe them to begin with. Without hope, how can they pick themselves up and move on? They can't, and they don't. They let the hardship become the focus of their lives, which chokes out any chance for joy. They remain locked in the pit of despair and depression because they have nothing to grasp to help pull them out.

Then there are those who let their hardships define them. These are the people who have anger so deeply etched on their faces that it is easily recognizable when you see them. They have focused on their circumstances for so long that they cannot see their lives any other way. They are angry, defiant, and lack self-respect, which often rears its head in countless other negative ways. We see this on the faces of the abused, of the poor, of the destitute. They have lived in less-than-desirable circumstances their whole lives and don't realize that they have other options. They don't realize that they don't have to become products of their environment. They don't know anything different, so the menu of options is totally lost on them. They don't understand that they can be the key that unlocks the chains that have oppressed them for so long, and sadly the trend gets passed down from generation to generation.

Finally, there are those who face hardship and oppression head on and learn from them. They use the lessons from those situations to get better, not bitter. These are the people who keep on getting up no matter what hits them. These are the people who focus on gratitude for what they have instead of focusing on what they don't have. These are the glass-half-full people who can see a rainbow in spite of the storm. They inspire and lead through their strength and positive attitudes. These are the people who learn from anything that comes their way. They get knocked down, but they keep getting up. Their path may lead them to a chasm, yet they build a bridge to the other side.

There are days when it is difficult to even put one foot in front of the other and keep on going, but none of us will ever face anything that God cannot help us through. Philippians 4:13 (NIV) says, *I can do all things through Christ who strengthens me,* and in Deuteronomy 31:6 (NIV) we read, *Be strong and courageous. Do not be afraid or terrified because of them, for the Lord your God goes with you; he will never leave you nor forsake you.*

When you fall, get up. When you face hardship, press on. When you are knocked down, look up. It isn't over until you say it's over. You haven't failed until you stop trying. You can choose how to respond to your circumstances. You can let hardship destroy you. You can let it define you. You can let it strengthen you. What choice will you make? ☙

27

It's Not About Me

"Rejoice always, pray continually, give thanks in all circumstances; for this is God's will for you in Christ Jesus."

1 THESSALONIANS 5:16–18 (NIV)

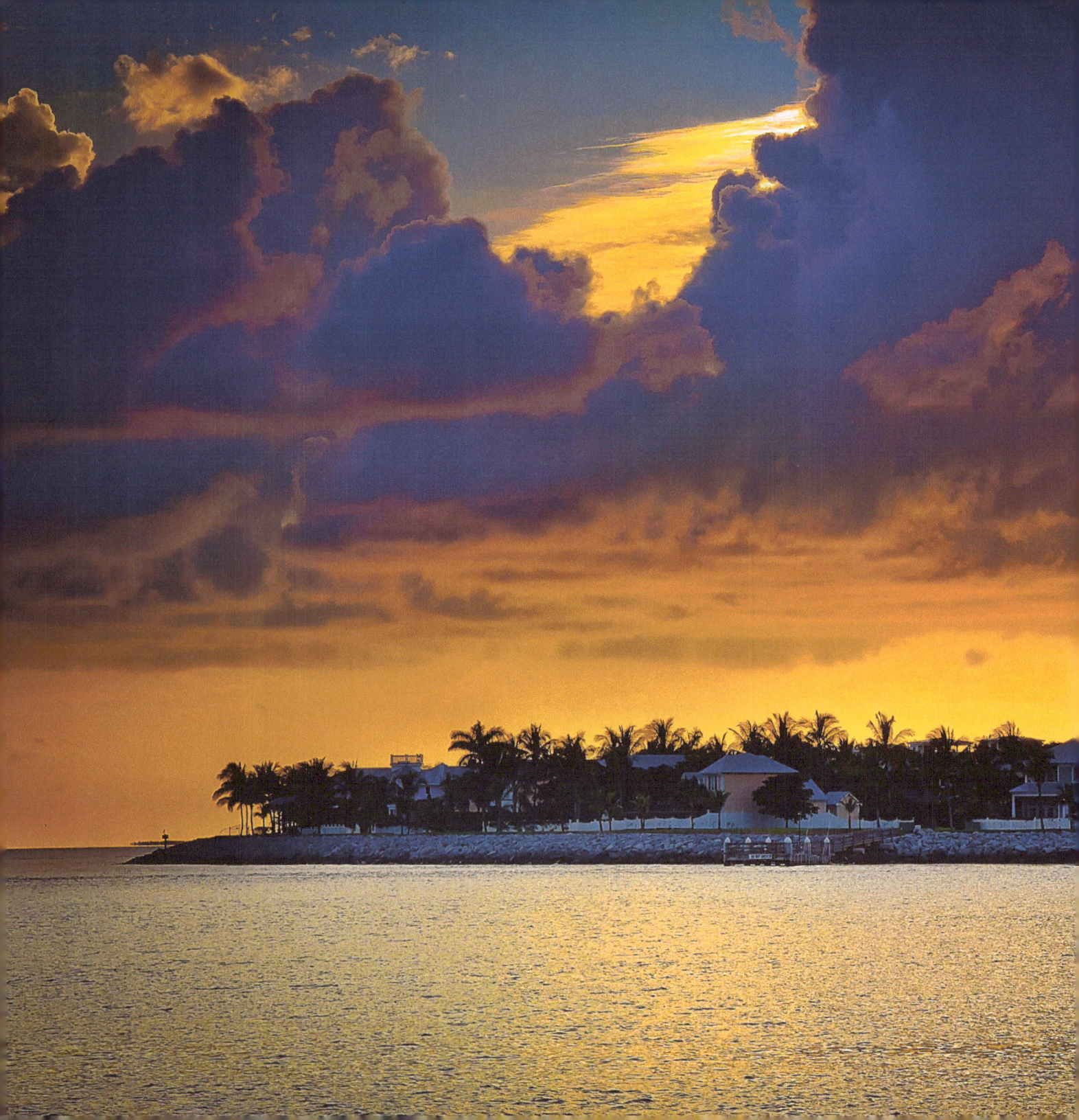

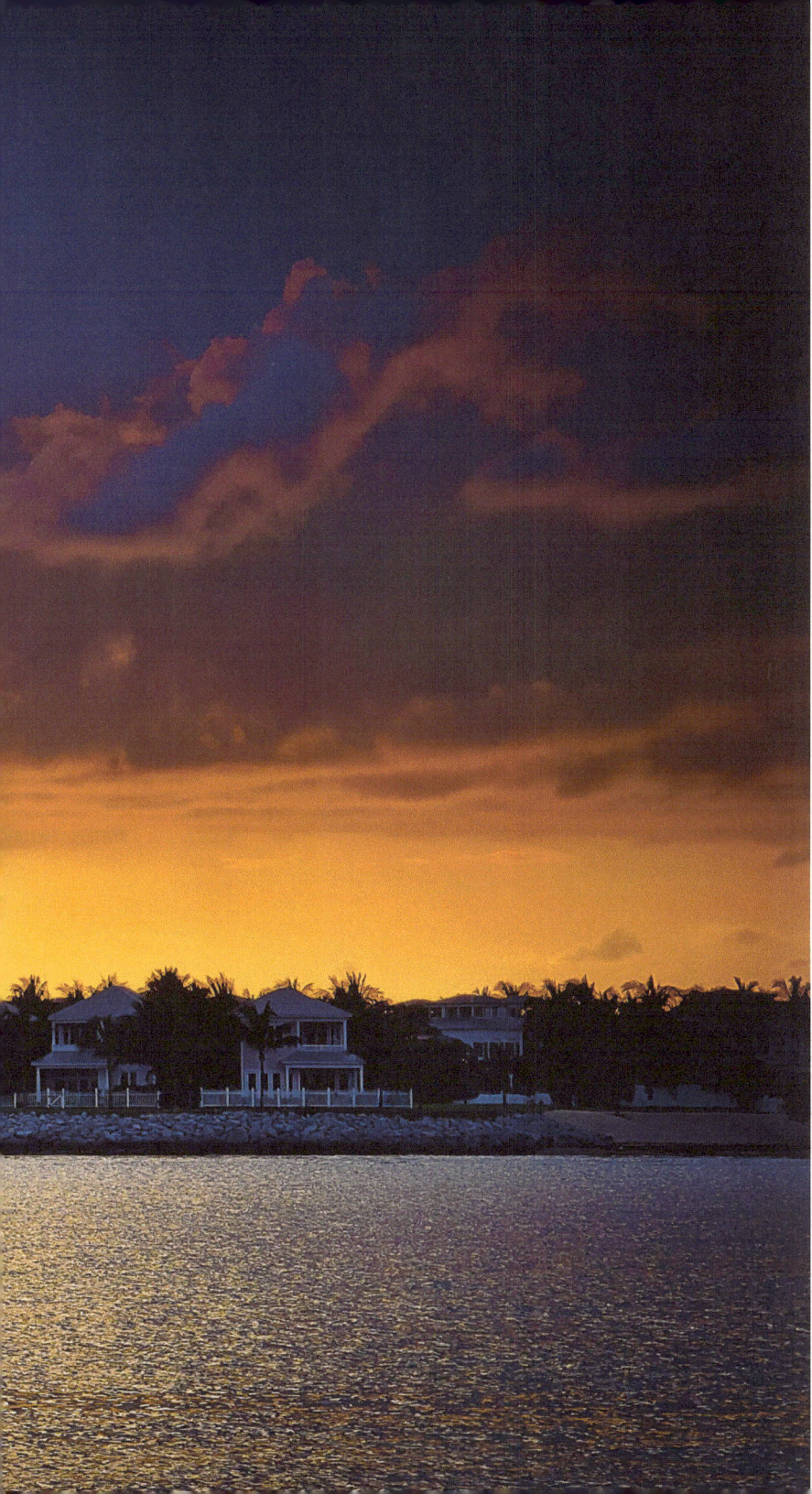

You can never get away from yourself.

Oh, sure, some people try. In an attempt to escape, they drink excessively, they take drugs, they pretend to be someone else, they immerse themselves in magazines about celebrities, they overload themselves with busyness so they don't have to think about anything else, they lose themselves in fiction novels, they try the latest and greatest product that hollowly promises a better life. All to no end. One simple truth remains: you can't get away from who you are.

Since we can't get away, it is easy to become so focused on ourselves that we can see nothing else. We look at our lives, and when we don't like what we see, we throw a pity party where we are the guests of honor. At times we are the only ones in attendance, while other times we invite everyone around us to attend. Do they want to be there? Not likely. Yet we include them anyway. We whine and complain about this or that, and we talk incessantly about the woes we are facing as if we are the only ones in the world who have ever gone through the fire. We lose sight of others so that, in our minds, we are the only ones that

SUNSET KEY RESORT,
KEY WEST, FLORIDA

matter. That line of thinking is "me" thinking. And that line of thinking is dangerous.

"Me" thinking will get you nowhere. It will not bring healing. It will not bring happiness. It will not ease your suffering. If anything, it yields the opposite. "Me" thinking brings misery to those who dwell in it, and it only yields more heartache because it does not offer reprieve or hope. "Me" thinking is self-centered and selfish and destructive.

But . . . it's not about me.

There are 7.3 billion people who inhabit this planet we call Earth. That's 7.3 billion living, breathing human beings with 7.3 billion different lives, each with their own set of problems. How then can we think that we are the only ones who have problems? That we are the only ones who have faced trials? In the grand scheme of things, we are merely a drop in a mighty big ocean. So, then, if we are so infinitesimal, what is our purpose in this giant world? Where do we fit?

We cannot see the grand scheme. Only God has the capacity to do that. Therefore, we need to trust that whatever He has chosen for us to endure must have a purpose. Is it possible that God is having us face trials and enduring circumstances because it will somehow build His kingdom? Is it possible that what we are going through now might someday be used to help someone else who is less equipped to deal with it than we? Is it possible that what we are facing today might serve a purpose for helping another person tomorrow? We cannot see the bigger picture the way that God sees it. We are merely drops in the ocean. We must trust Him to guide us through the waves.

In Acts 16, Paul and Silas meet a young slave woman who was afflicted with a spirit that allowed her to predict futures. She followed the two around for days, shouting, "These men are servants of the Most High God, who are telling you the way to be saved" (Acts 16:17, NIV). Her constant presence and outbursts eventually annoyed Paul enough that he commanded the spirit to leave her body, which it did. Because the slave's owners realized they could no longer make money from her talents, they dragged Paul and Silas to the authorities, where the two were bound, stripped, beaten, and thrown into prison. Paul and Silas could have moaned and complained and questioned "why me," but that is not how they responded. Instead, we read in verse 25 how they sang and prayed to God despite their circumstances. The other prisoners watched and listened. A little while later, a violent earthquake shook the prison, and all the prison doors flew open, and the prison chains came loose. The jailer, fearing all the prisoners had escaped and that he would suffer greatly from this travesty, drew his sword to end his life. Paul, however, stopped him by yelling, "Don't harm yourself! We are all here!" (Acts 16:28, NIV). Seeing this was true, the jailer asked, "Sirs, what must I do to be saved?" (Acts 16:29, NIV). Before the night was over, the jailer and his family were added to the numbers of believers.

Had Paul and Silas been afflicted with "me" thinking, that story would have had an entirely different ending. Instead of focusing on themselves and their less-than-ideal situation, they remained steadfast through their circumstances, and God used them to further His kingdom. How many times have we missed an opportunity like this because we failed to praise God in the midst of our trials, or because we placed the focus where it was never intended to be? Sometimes God allows us to go through trials because of the outcome it can yield if we keep our eyes on Him.

So the next time you are tempted to throw a pity party for yourself, think about it this way: It's not about me. It's about what I can do to help others. It's about who God needs me to be for the sake of someone else. ❧

28

A Single Drop of Rain

"From him the whole body, joined and held together by every supporting ligament, grows and builds itself up in love, as each part does its work."

EPHESIANS 4:16 (NIV)

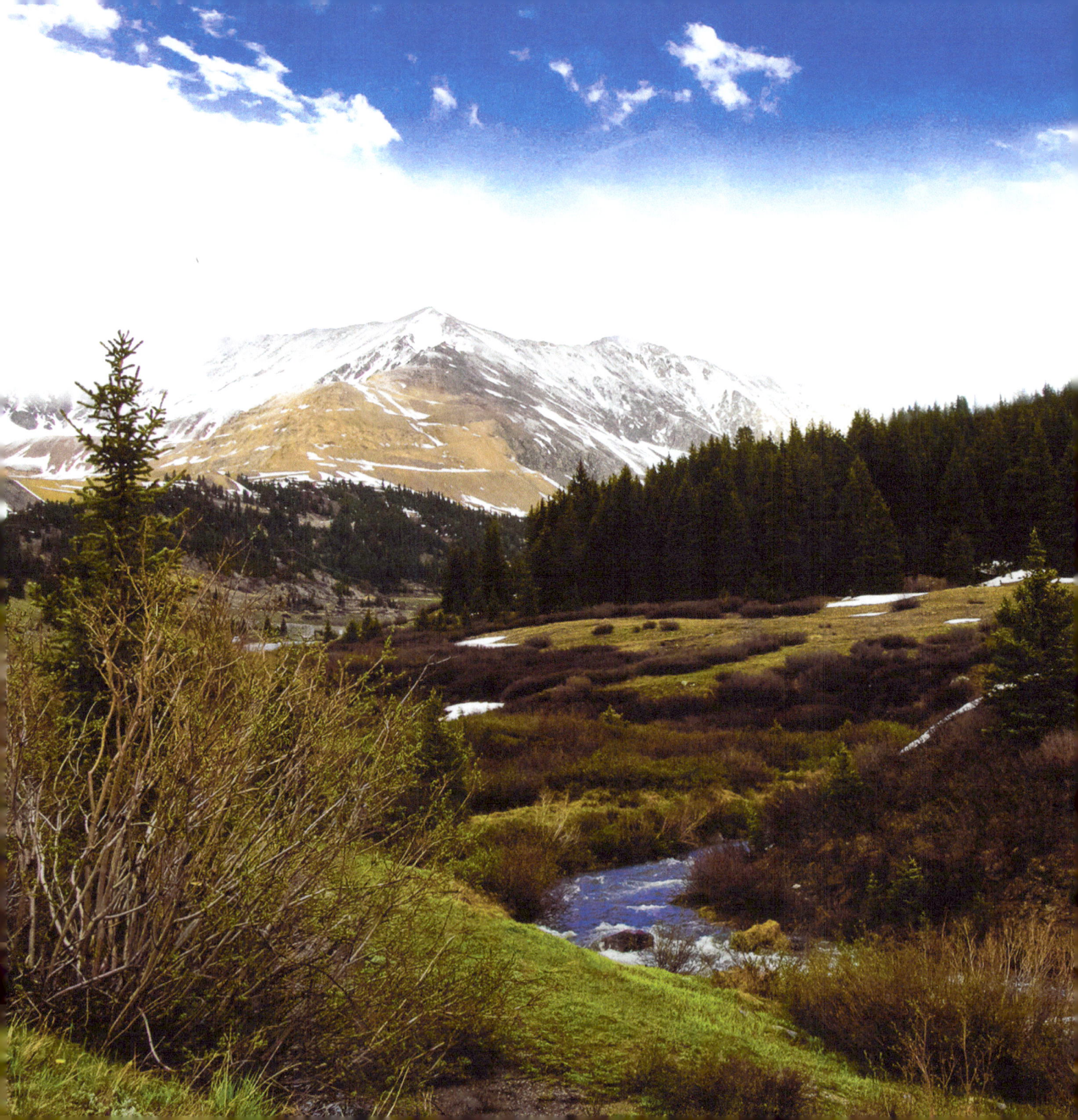

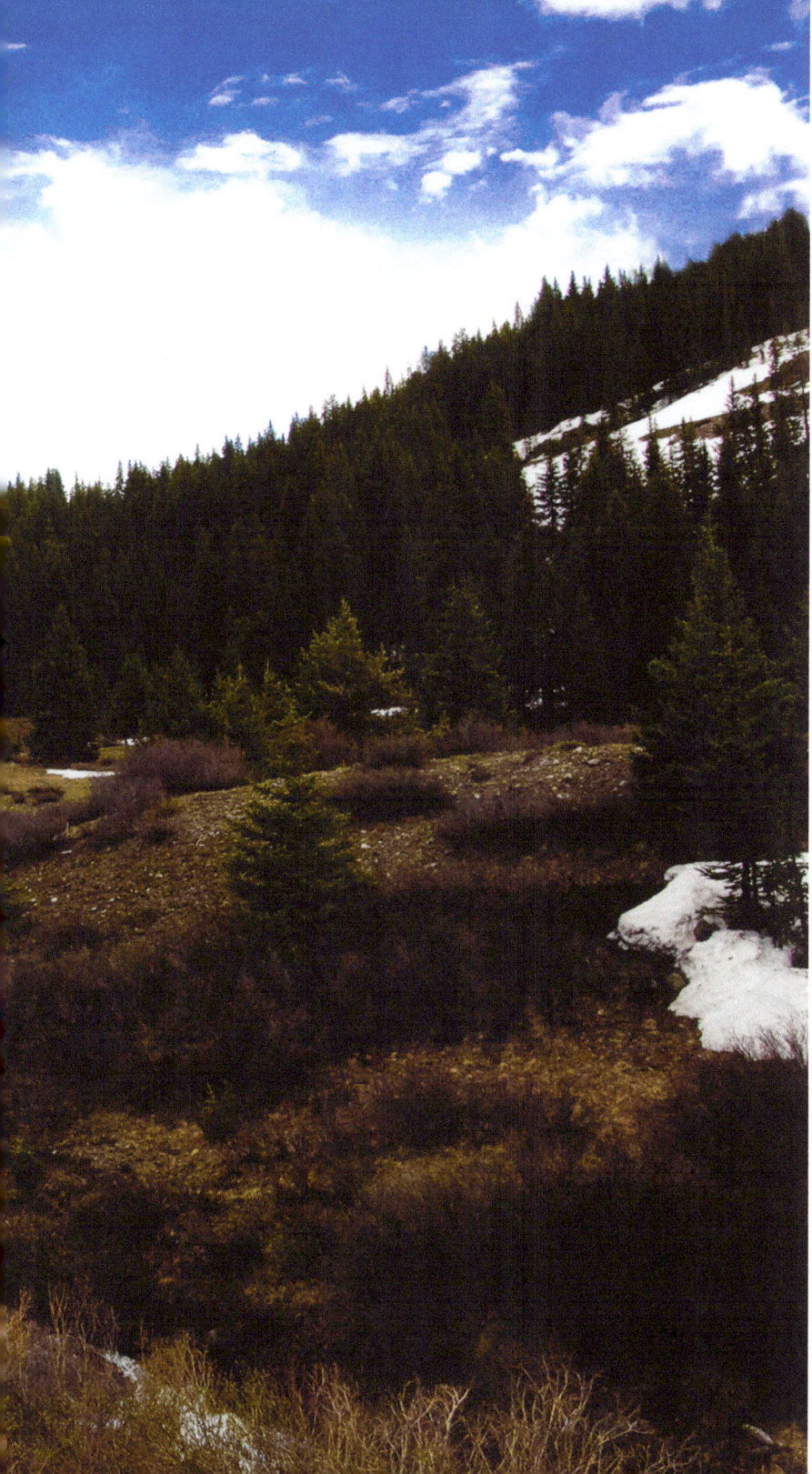

If you have ever been to the Grand Canyon in northern Arizona, you have witnessed one of the most amazing feats of nature.

Carved by the mighty Colorado River, the Grand Canyon runs a length of 277 miles, spans a width of 18 miles at its widest, and rises 6,093 feet from the floor of the canyon at its deepest point. Scientists estimate that the canyon's beginnings started over 17 million years ago. Over time, soil and rock succumbed to the forces of the swift-moving Colorado River, and the basin was chiseled away bit by bit.

What is interesting, however, is how docile the Colorado River is at its inception. The river originates at La Poudre Pass in Rocky Mountain National Park, about 25 miles north of Lake Granby. This mighty source of power begins as a tiny stream draining a simple, wet meadow. As it runs its course, the change

HEADWATERS OF THE ARKANSAS RIVER, LAKE COUNTY, COLORADO

in elevation and the addition of other rivers and streams join forces to create one of the most powerful water sources on Earth. This simple stream takes on new meaning when joined by other forces.

Our lives aren't much different. We start out small, weak, and simple. Left completely on our own, we wouldn't amount to much. But God planned our humble beginnings for so much more. He put us in the nurturing arms of caring mothers and fathers. He places people in our lives to join forces with us, and as time wears on, we gain strength and courage as we grow and mature. With maturity comes the ability to make a difference.

Let me put it another way. Let's imagine that each of us is a drop of water. Alone, we cannot do much. We cannot give nourishment to a parched land; we cannot fill lakes; we cannot carve canyons. If we focused only on our ability to do something as a single drop of water, we could accomplish nothing. If we looked at the other drops of water as insignificant or less important, we would evaporate into nothingness. Together, however, we can move mountains.

Ephesians 4 lays out the truth of how much we need one another. Each of us has a part to do, and we must carry out the work of that part to the best of our ability. If one of us chooses to sit back and let the others do the work, the strength of the whole weakens.

To clarify this, think in terms of the river . . . if the smaller streams felt they were insignificant because they were not as swift or as wide, and chose not to join forces with the main arm of the river, the whole of the river would suffer. When that happens, the force of the water lessens and canyons cannot be carved.

In 1 Corinthians 12 (NIRV) we read, "*Suppose the foot says, 'I am not a hand. So I don't belong to the body.' By saying this, it cannot stop being part of the body. And suppose the ear says, 'I am not an eye. So I don't belong to the body.' By saying this, it cannot stop being part of the body. If the whole body were an eye, how could it hear? If the whole body were an ear, how could it smell? God has placed each part in the body just as he wanted it to be. If all the parts were the same, how could there be a body? As it is, there are many parts. But there is only one body.*"

When we, like single drops of rain, join forces with one another and carry out the work we were created to do, we become greater than the sum of our parts. We become one body created to further the Kingdom of God. We become mighty rivers, and we gain the power to carve canyons. ❧

ABOUT THE AUTHOR

Deborah DeJong was born in 1960 and has lived in rural Iowa all her life. Raised in a Christian home, she has followed Christ since early childhood. She graduated from William Penn College, Oskaloosa, Iowa, with a bachelor of arts degree in education in 1981, and obtained a master's degree in education from Viterbo University, LaCrosse, Wisconsin, in 2006. Deborah has been a middle school teacher since 1991—teaching English/language arts for eighteen years and technology classes for the remaining years. After introducing digital photography into her technology curriculum, she discovered a passion for the art of photography and continues to hone her photography skills. Deborah specializes in the art of landscape photography, but does not limit herself to that type of photography. She has also developed a small portrait photography clientele and frequently takes family, senior, and wedding portraits. Deborah has been married to her husband Dave since 1979, has two children and three grandchildren, and currently resides in Oskaloosa, Iowa.

BIBLIOGRAPHY

Southerland, Mary. "Speak No Evil." Girlfriends in God Blog. Accessed April 6, 2016. http://girlfriendsingod.com/speak-no-evil

Merriam-Webster. "Thanks." Accessed April 6, 2016. http://www.merriam-webster.com/dictionary/thanks